DANCING
AT THE
STILL POINT

Marion Woodman, SOPHIA, and Me
A Friendship Remembered

by Elinor Dickson

CHIRON PUBLICATIONS • ASHEVILLE, NORTH CAROLINA

www.ChironPublications.com

Interior and cover design by Danijela Mijailovic
Printed primarily in the United States of America.

ISBN 978-1-63051-695-6 paperback
ISBN 978-1-63051-696-3 hardcover
ISBN 978-1-63051-697-0 electronic
ISBN 978-1-63051-698-7 limited edition paperback

Library of Congress Cataloging-in-Publication Data Pending

FOR ALL THE FRIENDS WHO HAVE LOVED,
SUPPORTED AND CHALLENGED US

The immense fulfillment of the friendships between those
engaged in furthering the evolution of consciousness has a
quality almost impossible to describe.

Teilhard de Chardin

Except for the point, the still point,
There would be no dance, and there is only the dance.

T. S. Eliot, Four Quartets

TABLE OF CONTENTS

ACKNOWLEDGMENTS

Thank you
to the many friends and clients I travelled with
and who so generously shared their stories;
to Lindy Hough for her suggestions;
to Diane Patterson, who made me a better writer;
to Anne, Andrea, Maria, Rosemary,
and Wendy for their encouragement;
to Barbara Joy for her support, experience in
writing memoir and formatting computers;
to Len Cruz and Jennifer Fitzgerald for their enthusiastic support,
and to Danijela Mijailovic for the wonderful designs;
and finally, to Sophia, whose illumination surfaced
so many times in the writing of this book.

PREFACE

This book was born out of a dream; a dream in which Marion instructed me to write about our friendship "so others might gain from it." These are words I continue to ponder. During the spring and summer of 2015, I shared this manuscript with Marion. One day, as we took turns reading to each other, Marion declared, "This is a spiritual document." I realized that was true. What I have learned in writing this book is that our friendship, like all friendships rooted in the Self, in the heart of Sophia, allows the emerging field to come into consciousness in a way that is supported and enhanced by what is coming through each person. In turn, this shared energy becomes the foundation of community, an alchemical vessel capable of bringing forth a new creation.

Marion and I met in the second half of life, at a time when we had both pierced through to the realm of Beingness. This realm has been given many names: God, Self, Source, Mystery, the Tao, or the Implicate Order, but for us, it is a dynamic presence that we experience as Love, the eternal creative process seeking to bring the world into being. In recognizing this creative principle as feminine wisdom, we knew that our lives are not really ours but the gift of Sophia, the source of all manifestation wanting to emerge through us. Our relationship deepened as we *saw* each other through the eyes of that love, and in the many ways we mirrored each other; being challenged to grow into the *experience* of such love was the most profound gift of our friendship. As we dared to engage each other with increasing levels of transparency and authenticity, we realized Sophia was not only weaving the field within and between us but weaving the field around us. Our relationship was not only personally supportive, but it supported a deepening understanding of a new worldview based on the emerging realization of the interconnectedness between women, men, and all of creation. Exploring the feminine principle as the basis for the next revolution in consciousness, we came to understand the destiny we were each given through dreams and our life process. Early on, Marion was given the task of writing a "new book;" an articulation of an emerging feminine consciousness buried in our recorded history. My task was to bring the great monster, "the weight of human history," up from the depths "so the water can flow again." The release of the feminine principle of creative presence, process and interconnectedness, of true "globalization," became part of our shared destiny.

In writing this book, I have endeavored to remain faithful to the soul/spirit axis letting the dream flow through me and evolve into its own structures. Like many dreams, the result is more thematic than chronological as our journey wove its way through the vicissitudes of time.

Part I tells of our individual encounters with Self/Sophia, the archetype of wholeness, and our meeting at the still point, that place where the personal and the transpersonal intersect.

Part II contains reflections on our interpersonal dance, what we shared, how we played, how we dealt with shadow material, and how we contained and witnessed each other over 30-plus years.

Part III comprises a snapshot of our interactions with the world that constellated around us and the many discussions we had that helped to articulate our experience. As one surrenders to Sophia, "the continuous process within the eternal," you can no longer tell the dancer from the dance. Our discussions, our work, our experiences became a visible expression of the tapestry of our friendship and our individual destinies.

Finally, **Part IV** I see as "coming home"; friendship in old age as we prepared for the last dance.

INTRODUCTION

I have always resonated with a statement by Professor David Clark who wrote of Marion, "Woodman's life is larger than the designs that would explain it."[1] While I was aware Marion had told several people I understood her and her work probably better than anyone, given their scope, it never entered my mind to write about her, and in particular, to write about our friendship. That possibility changed in late November 2014 when I awoke with a very clear dream.

I am making my way through a labyrinth of streets, deserted except for a few rough-looking and menacing men. In spite of feeling threatened, I walk past them and come to a door where Marion is staying. A woman opens the door and lets me in. She tells me Marion is upstairs but to be very gentle, the implication being that Marion is not well. I stand quietly at the bottom of the stairs for a few minutes, opening myself to Sophia and asking for Her guidance to come forth in me. Ascending the stairs, I find Marion in a large nightgown, curled up on top of the bed. When I enter she immediately sits up. Fully alert she exclaims, "You must write a book about our friendship. People will gain from it."

---

[1] Clark, David (2005). The Last Temptation of Marion Woodman. In *Body and Soul: Honoring Marion Woodman, Spring Journal.*

All morning, the dream kept reverberating through my body. Arriving at the kitchen, a large pot of tea seemed in order. How would I even begin such a task? Although we had known each other for a few years previously, we became friends when I was 46 and Marion was 57. Ours was a relationship born in the second half of life. When we met, Marion had completed a 23-year career as a high school English teacher. Her second career took her to Zurich, at first for her own health reasons, but she stayed and became a Jungian analyst. Six years after returning to Toronto, she had just published her third book and had a large private practice. I had been a clinical psychologist for 16 years, and the last six years were spent building a psychology department at an inner-city trauma hospital. Working outside the hospital, I gave many lectures and workshops on psychology, spirituality, and community as well as serving on Boards of Directors concerned with addiction and homelessness. There was little time for rest. Having achieved in the first half of life what many might see as success, we were, each in our own way, compelled to enter the dark wood of midlife to face the hidden, shadowy depths of our psyche. By 1985, "the year of our friendship," we had broken through to that place of Beingness, realizing that our lives are not really ours but the gift of Sophia's life within us.

By my second cup of tea, the questions presenting themselves were "why did we meet, and why did we meet at this time?" Nothing is really by chance. Images flashed through my mind, shifting and changing like a kaleidoscope. Certainly, our relationship embodied great affect; we laughed a lot, we argued, even fought on at least one occasion, and we felt each other's joy and pain. Above all, our friendship embodied the intensity with which we lived our individual lives. In the continuing emergence of the soul, we were both witness and container for each other. It was as if it were destined. Maybe that was the key! Looking out my kitchen window at the November trees clutching their last remaining leaves, my memory took flight to the 2010 film based on Marion's life. Her opening words focused on the fact that "we all have a destiny." Whether our destiny is expressed in raising a child, creating a dance, or saving a forest, we know it is something we "must" do. Destiny gives life its meaning and is often revealed in the threads that connect our life. The essay we wrote at 13 is mirrored in the thesis we wrote at 33 or the work we are engaged in now.

Deep down, we all retain a memory of being part of something greater than ourselves and once embraced, our individual destiny becomes part of an emerging mosaic of the whole. Like many people, Marion and I did not fully comprehend our destiny until we were in our 50s, but once our destiny became clear, we realized that everything in our lives, before and after, is a circumambulation of the soul's evolutionary spiral.

Destiny is not just an idea or something we can construct. If we try, it will swallow us. True destiny rises unannounced from within and as such can be equally exhilarating, terrifying, and deeply humbling. To fulfill our destiny, the ego, our organ of consciousness, can do nothing but wait in attentive surrender until slowly we realize that Sophia, the "Self" organizing energy at the heart of all creation is transforming us. While our soul's destiny is forged in solitude, we are not left orphans. We are given friends, our true companions, for the journey. For Marion and me, our destinies were intertwined, and for the past 30-plus years, so too were our lives. Since my 20s, I was aware of having surrendered my life to a process I could barely understand. What a joy to find someone who could meet me at the crossroads.

In Marion's words, "destiny is the life we owe to the soul"; therefore, I have attempted to write this book from that deep soul place. The soul is seldom linear or predictable, preferring to speak through the images in our dreams or through the affect that gives rise to the synchronistic connections in our lives. Finishing my tea, I went to the computer and, as in the morning's dream, I surrendered to what wanted to come through me. I was going to London to see Marion in two days, so I would lay the "situation" before her. As in the dream, when I entered her room, she was sitting upright in bed—nursing a sore toe. She surged forward with arms outstretched. Following lunch, we settled in. I read the first five pages of what I had written. Marion was becoming weaker, but she always amazed me when we get to dreams and process. She was right there, eyes shining, fully engaged and making comments—even correcting my sentence structure at one point! The thing is, she didn't let me off the hook! We both agreed that anything sentimental or self-indulgent would be worthless, but we equally knew I wouldn't be disposed to write anything of that nature. Our relationship, so deeply personal, is transpersonal, and if I managed to stay with essence, it might have some merit in the telling.

Relationship rooted in commitment to Self/Sophia does not exist for its own sake. While each person needs to pursue their unique destiny in that clear, unpeopled space, synchronicity, the hallmark of soul/spirit relationship, magically weaves patterns of mutual insight and support. In this way, we not only become a part of each other's destiny, but the energy spirals outward affecting the world around us. So, every morning, with Marion's words, "you must follow the dream" ringing in my ears, I made my way through the "menacing maze of intimidating men" and leaving my doubts behind, sat at my computer. Across 30-plus years, I hope these memories of a friendship forged through a shared destiny will invite you to enter, not only into our journey, but also to reflect on your own soul's journey and those who travel with you.

PART I

MEETING AT
THE STILL POINT

ONE

Relationship has to do with the exquisitely tuned harmonics between two people who are attempting to become conscious of their personal psychology. The mystery of each individual is holy, and the mystery which brings each into relationship with the other is tenuous, invisible, and sacred.

Marion

On a Wednesday at 3 p.m. in the early spring of 1985, Marion and I became friends. Three o'clock marked the time of my weekly appointment for analysis. In fact, that day marked my 49th session. As usual, I walked into the office totally energized and focused. Marion stood there looking at me quite intently. Finally, she said, "You don't need analysis. I think the reason we got together is that we're meant to be friends." As she waited for my reaction, I could only laugh. I recited the dream I had upon awakening that morning.

I was walking down a cobblestone street when an enormous wind came and picked me up depositing me under a portico. It was the door to Jung's office. A woman opened the door and I went through Jung's office into an inner courtyard that was Marion's office, open to the sky with a floor of grass. I sat on the sofa while Marion went into Jung's office and brought back grapes and wine. We talked. Then it was time for me to go. I looked around and thought I saw some fleeting shadows on the television but when I went over it was unplugged. Marion accompanied me outside. As we were walking to my car a young woman, Mary, came to the door to tell me I had a long-distance phone call. I went back to take it and the message was, "The analyst is dead." The grass had the same texture and undulation as the floor in the office. We sat down and continued talking.

My analysis is over. The "analyst" is dead. Years later, Marion couldn't believe how bold she was. "I can't imagine saying that to an analysand!" Yet, as was usually the case, her intuition was right on. Through my dream, the unconscious gave us the assurance that there were few, if any, projections floating around the room. The television had no shadows. In fact, it wasn't even plugged into an energy source. The grass floor of the office and the grass outside had virtually the same contours. Continuity was assured. We simply sat down on the grass and resumed talking; a conversation that lasted for over 30 years.

On a warm summer day in 2014, Marion, analyst Wendy Willmot, and I went for a picnic in Gibbons Park where we were joined by Ann Skinner, Marion's longtime friend and colleague, and her friend, Linda, a dancer from Montreal. Seeing her beloved Annie striding across the grass, Marion became her playful self, and we had a joyous time doing our own version of Shakespeare in the Park. Later, sitting over tea in the courtyard of the Villa, conversation turned to the people Marion had me do various forms of body and voice work with during my analysis so long ago. The story of my 49-hour analysis and even shorter termination came up. Head bent, Marion became very quiet, working her fingers as she did when she was formulating a deep insight. Looking up she said, "Everything I was working on and moving toward was sitting there every week in the chair across from me."

I know the depth of our friendship, so I wasn't totally surprised by her statement but in that moment, I was humbled. Now as then, she always *saw* me. On returning to Toronto, I was inspired to look up exactly what she was working on and writing about at that time. It didn't take very long for the core of our relationship to become apparent.

Marion in her office on St. Clair Avenue, 1987 from Jung Foundation Newsletter (photographer unknown).

Elinor at her desk at St. Michael's Hospital, 1987 from the Toronto Star (photographer unknown).

TWO

Making a commitment to another is really an illusion, a way of holding. Seeking a greater realization of the Self is the only commitment we can *really* make.

Marion and Elinor

The seeds of our friendship burst into life the first time I met Marion in 1983. I was part of an overflowing crowd that had come to hear her speak at the University of Toronto. When she walked out on stage, my soul almost pulled my body out of the chair. I knew instantly this was the person who would be my guide for the next stage of my journey. For the first time, at the age of 44, I was suddenly remembering my dreams; dreams involving earthquakes, fire, tidal waves. While on the surface my life was going well, my unconscious was erupting with immense force.

Those explosive dreams led me to Carl Jung and Marie Louise von Franz, whose works I read voraciously. But reading Jung and going into analysis are two different things. During the six months I waited for Marion to work me into her practice, I gave a talk at a large alcohol addiction center where I was given a book, *Addiction to Perfection*, as a gift. After reading what would become Marion's best-selling work, I couldn't wait for my first appointment. I awoke that morning with a pre-analysis dream, a dream that often outlines what the work will be about. My three-part dream pointed to my need to integrate body and soul. Unerringly, I was led to the right person! Marion also wanted to know about the dreams I had on the three consecutive nights that brought me into analysis; earth, fire, and water erupting all around me. "You must have gotten very ill," she said. How did she know that? I looked at her in amazement! I was about to learn that if you don't pay attention to your dreams, your body will get through to you in a more direct way.

I told Marion the story of my driving over two hours to give a talk at an event that had been planned for some time. I didn't feel well, but there were about 200 people coming so I carried on. By the time of the talk I had lost my voice almost completely and had to whisper across a microphone to make myself heard. While I managed to drive home, morning necessitated a call to Peter, a physician friend of mine, who diagnosed pleurisy. Breathing caused excruciating pain. Yes, my body wasn't going to take any more. My first introduction to body/soul! Marion explained that there was more spirit than the body could contain. She was right. Feeling that I had been given much, I wanted to give back. I was living out of an ideal that my body could no longer sustain.

Marion wanted to know the passion that was driving me, and I knew from her writing and lectures I could talk freely about the parts of my life I rarely discussed. In 1970, and about to go off to pursue a Ph.D. in Clinical Psychology, I decided to make a 28-day retreat. At the age of 31 and well-practiced in meditation, I found that every time I began to meditate I was taken up into an intense white light, so intense that I knew if I didn't return I would die. My body could not take the energy. A well-known Jesuit spiritual director from the University of Madrid happened to be passing through so I went to talk with him. After some reflection, he encouraged me to forego such satori experiences, as I was not yet ready for such an influx of light. To remedy this, I had to avoid my usual meditation. A few days later, I was relaxing in a Muskoka chair on the brow of a hill when suddenly I had a vision of a large group of people coming up from the valley led by a glorious figure dressed in white and gold. My culturally informed consciousness saw this figure as Christ. He stood before me and asked for my hand in marriage. I was terrified and spent the night on my knees in a candle-lit chapel before my heart could stammer out a "yes." During the three weeks that followed, I seemed to live in, what I would now call, the Imaginal Realm; that place between subjective and objective reality. While I managed to eat, sleep, and function normally, I did not know whether I was in the body or out of the body. "Let him kiss me with kisses of his mouth! More delightful is your love than wine." The Old Testament Canticle of Canticles became a living reality. The ravishment was complete. Now a distant memory, the intensity of that encounter nearly 50 years ago still remains.

The other advice the Spanish spiritual director gave me was by way of introducing me to the Spanish mystic, Teresa of Avila. Through her writings, she would be my guide for the next 14 years. In 1984, along with my dreams of earth, fire, and water, I had another pre-analysis dream where I entered a walled garden. Sitting on a chair in the middle of the garden was a woman dressed in the garb of a Carmelite. Naturally, I thought it was Teresa of Avila but as I got closer, I recognized the analyst, Dr. Marie Louise von Franz. Sometimes my unconscious has a dry sense of humor, but I got the message—my inner guide was about to change. I was about to learn things about the dynamics of the inner life beyond where Teresa could take me.

The juxtaposing of these two figures is not as big a leap as it might seem. Teresa had a dry, almost irreverent sense of humor, loved to dance, and managed to stay one step ahead of the Spanish Inquisition in writing about the spiritual life. In trying to express the inexpressible, Teresa, well aware of the numinous energy she was dealing with, introduced symbols and metaphor to catch the nuances of the body/soul/spirit journey. The interior castle was a round, crystal palace, and through a spiraling fashion, one moved deeper into its seven mansions or stages of transformation. She often used the symbol of the butterfly to talk about these transformations and the fact that as we draw closer to the light the snakes and demons, our hidden shadow side, comes into view. For Teresa, knowledge of self is knowledge of God. No matter how advanced a person is in the spiritual life, the one thing this mystical doctor of the church insisted upon was the need to grow daily in self-knowledge. Writers, such as John Welch, O.C., see Teresa as a 16th century precursor of Jung.

During my analysis, there were a few times when I thought, with some amusement, that she was sitting across from me.

Bernini's sculpture of St. Teresa in Ecstasy presented in Addiction to Perfection. *Public Domain.*

The year that Marion came to Toronto to set up her practice at 223 St. Clair Avenue coincided with the most defining year in my life. I call 1979, the year of my 40th birthday, my Jericho year. That is, the whole year seemed to be a circumambulation around a core event that necessitated the tumbling down of many walls. It started with meeting Thomas Berry and an invitation to join him in facilitating a weeklong series of seminars to a group of 40 religious leaders from across the country. Over that week, Thomas and I had self-contained suites across the hall from each other. In the evenings we usually met to talk over the day, and it was during this time he challenged me to approach psychology in a way similar to his approach to theology. As a "geologian," his favorite term for himself, he saw everything in the broad spectrum of evolution. He talked about the four scriptures: the cosmic scriptures, the verbal scriptures, the historical scriptures, and the scriptures written in the very structure of our being. While it was the "scriptures written in the very structure of our being" that had led to my choosing psychology over theology 10 years earlier, now Thomas presented me with a vastly deeper and wider view.

A second crack in the wall of my worldview came through an invitation from my friend Peter to take a physics course at the University of Toronto in 1978-79. The revolution in physics was seeping into the collective mind-set, and there was a demand on the part of many people to understand the implications of these developments. This was a course designed for those lacking advanced mathematical skill, but over the year, I learned about Schrodinger's cat, double-slit experiments, complementarity, the uncertainty principle, parallel universes, and many other mind-expanding theories and experiments.

This course had two major impacts on my life that would shape my future journey both as a psychologist and as a person. In the first place, since graduating with a Ph.D. in clinical psychology, while I found myself vaguely unsatisfied with the whole underlying premise of psychology, I was hard-pressed to articulate this dissatisfaction. In studying quantum mechanics, I realized that psychology was not keeping pace with the rest of science. It was still operating out of a Newtonian model. Newton's model is correct and necessary in many ways. We could not go to the moon without it. The same is true for psychology. Neuropsychology, cognitive/behavioral therapy, personality testing, and other techniques have much to recommend, and I have used them quite successfully on many occasions. But our under-standing of the human being still had its roots in Pavlov and Skinner, in the bits and pieces of humanity, not in the whole. Our psyche cannot be *limited* to brain chemistry or early childhood development or personality measured against statistical norms. When the quantum worldview is laid over the Newtonian world, new possibilities emerge. I realized this was the underlying premise I had been looking for, a door into a four-dimensional world.

Secondly, the physics professor teaching the course would, on several occasions, make reference to Carl Jung. As a psychologist I had heard of Jung—barely. He is certainly not taught in most graduate schools. Similarly, the small introduction to Jung in my physics class might have slipped by except for the fact that Thomas Berry was writing to me from New York and sending me some of his early papers. On one occasion he wrote: "The immediate future will be a period of regression into the deeper self, a return to the archetypal world. Indeed, one of the functions fulfilled by the modern psychologies of the unconscious is to prepare contemporary man for this mythic journey into the future and the past."[2] The modern "psychologies of the *unconscious*" were not anything I had heard about in graduate school.

By May of 1979, my mind was liberated. A new worldview was taking shape in me, an evolutionary worldview that stretched across the mists of time; an invisible world of waves and fields; a world that could not be pigeon-holed and held captive by my rational mind. The walls that came down brought into sharp focus how literal both religion and science had become. At their extremes they are like warriors behind concrete bastions hurling distortions at each other across a wasteland. Finally, the spirit in me found room to blow where it would. Tennyson's "margin that fades forever and forever when I move" became a reality and I was moving toward that distant horizon walking on a cloud of uncertainty. It was exhilarating.

I still remember the huge energy that reverberated throughout my body at the possibilities before me. With Irene, a friend and

---

[2] Berry, Thomas, from an essay sent to me in 1980 entitled, "Future Forms of Religious Experience," (p. 4).

colleague, this same energy carried me to France in late May of 1979. We had no agenda but spent the following weeks traversing Europe. My friend was quite cosmopolitan, speaking several languages; I was the dumb-struck tourist on my first visit to the Continent. Our adventures left us with many, often hilarious, stories. Of the five days we spent in Paris, apart from some incredible meals, it was walking into Notre Dame Cathedral with the light streaming through the great Rose Windows that left me breathless. Equally stirring my energy were the Impressionists. What I saw in those paintings was light shining through matter. I suddenly realized that, like the new physics, this art depicted a perception of the world beyond the causal notions of time and space.

Walking by the train station, we noticed that the Orient Express was leaving the next day. What better way to get to Venice. After Venice came Florence to be followed by Rome, where we "accidently" had an audience with the newly elected Pope, John Paul II. It was here in the eternal city that I turned 40. After a week, and since we were on that side of the Atlantic, we decided to go to Africa. In contrast to the museums, art, and architecture of Europe, here the natural beauty left me dazzled; brilliant skies and air perfumed from copious flowering trees and bushes seemed to embrace us. After the first week, however, my journey took on a different meaning.

There is an old spiritual saying: You must die before you die. In my case, I awoke in the middle of the night with everything swimming before my eyes. I hovered in a twilight zone until morning when Irene discovered me in a semi-conscious state. A doctor was called for. He arrived and though he spoke no English, we managed to communicate. After a quick examination, he wrote out five prescriptions and called for a young boy to go to the village and have them filled. I gave him money and, I must confess, entertained the thought of whether or not I would see him or the money again. To my lasting shame, he ran all the way there and back proffering the medication—and the change. While an IV was not possible, medication was put in a large jar of water which I had to sip on continuously. This, along with five other prescriptions, cured my parasitic poisoning. Another week and I was able to take the long journey home.

When I was lucid during that long night, I went into panic at the thought of never seeing my family again, not completing my work, not knowing what would become of me in this foreign place. Having no control over what would happen, I slowly began to surrender, to let go of my agenda. In my semi-conscious state, what came to me were the words of the poet Rilke: "Only from the side of death is it possible to do justice to love."[3] It took those little parasites to teach me about non-attachment to people, places, and things. I had to truly let go. A surrendered heart is the foundation of love, and in the permeable boundary between life and death, this was the lesson I had to learn.

The physical manifestation of being near death was only one of several deaths I underwent that year. We die into death or we die into life. Dying into life always entails the death of the ego's agenda; the habitual thought patterns, the scripted feelings we learn from our parents, our friends, our culture, need to be made permeable. We need to step, or be forced, outside the box to gain a greater view of reality. This is very different from the ego that is possessed by an ideal. Ideals, like ideologies, can seem like expansion but they easily devolve into further rigidities in disguise. For a greater reality to emerge in us, our perceptions of space and time must be altered. Bringing down the walls that once defined my understanding of myself and the world was, I believe, necessary in opening me to a defining encounter with Source.

One evening in late August that year, at a cottage north of Toronto, I was reflecting on the shadow places within my psyche. Suddenly, my personal reflection opened into a transpersonal abyss that all but encompassed me. Awake all night, I was gripped in total fear. Difficult to describe because of its intense feeling of chaos, it was a vision of the world without spirit, without consciousness—an apocalyptic nightmare of boiling oceans and crumbling mountains. The only distinct image that emerged was of someone caught in a whirlpool, completely submerged in the spiraling waters except for a bloodied hand reaching up and grasping a large rock. I realized that it

[3] Rilke, Rainer Maria. (2006). *Diuno Elegies*. New York, New York: W.W. Norton and Company.

was *my* hand. I was the person in the whirlpool. Amid the chaos that was swirling about me, all I could do was try and keep centered in consciousness. If my ego had not been strong and flexible enough to hold on, the onslaught of such unconscious forces might have left me psychotic.

After hours of exhausting visions of opposing forces, of the life and death of the universe, morning came, and I went out and stood looking at the lake. Standing at the water's edge and listening to the birds, it was as if I stepped outside of time and space and experienced *everything* connected in love; there was only love. Many times, I have tried to describe this experience to myself, but, essentially, it remains beyond words. At first, all of nature, myself included, shone with an iridescent glow, and then everything went beyond images. All sense of self disappeared. My mind, my being, was absorbed by a universal vibration, a state of being beyond anything imaginable. It was an experience of the unity behind all manifestation and that unity resonated within me as Love.

On that morning in 1979, as I came back into the realm of time and space, I walked over to the dining room to join the others for breakfast. Life goes on! I did not speak of my experience; it was too soon for words, but suddenly I *knew* what Meister Eckhart meant when he said that the ground of Being and the ground of our being are one and the same. I *knew* that the deepest point of interiority is also the hidden origin of creation. Over time, I would find resonance with this reality in many places. It carried me beyond the boundaries of familiar religious imagery and into the place experienced by poets and mystics across time. In the words of Krishnamurti, "Knowing, Knower, Known, are One"; or the poet Rumi who proclaimed, "you are the universe in ecstatic motion"; to Marion who knew, "the dancer is the dance."

The experiences of 1979 had to be processed and assimilated. Looking out from the Still Point, I knew I had to bring the treasure home into everyday reality. Nine months after my encounter with Thomas Berry I became an unofficial "writer-in-residence" with a large office overlooking a campus courtyard, courtesy of a generous friend and St. Michael's College at the University of Toronto. Thomas's evolutionary perspective and my own recent experience blew apart whatever assumptions I had about history, including the fact that history is linear. Of necessity, I found myself delving into almost every field of inquiry: cultural history, archaeology, anthropology, philosophy, science, and medicine. I began to see the deeper patterns in these diverse fields as they unfolded throughout time, eventually pointing to, I believe, the wound at the core of the modern psyche. I began recording my thoughts in a journal I labeled "The Wisdom Option."

An evolutionary perspective, particularly as it related to human development, had been largely missing from my formal education. Like most people, what I learned were mostly linear, causal events chronicled from a masculine point of view. Books such as Riane Eisler's *The Chalice and the Blade* would not be published for eight more years, but it seems the unconscious was stirring on many fronts. From my own research I realized for the first time that for much of our 2,000,000-year history we were fetal in the womb of creation until 230,000 years ago, when we emerged and carved an image of the Great Mother. In our act of carving an image, consciousness became self-reflective and our role as the conveyor of meaning in the diverse tapestry of evolution was defined. I came to understand the two major paradigms in human evolution and a third paradigm we were leaning into. That is, we went from an instinctual, magical self to an ego self; from tribal structures to hierarchical structures; from polytheism to monotheism; from power from nature to power against nature; from power as gift to power as strength; from a dependent state to an independent state. The first paradigm is often considered to have more fully emerged approximately 30,000 years ago, while the second paradigm emerged from 6–7,000 years ago. The first we called matriarchal and the second, patriarchal, but if further evolution was to occur, it became apparent to me we had to move into a vastly deeper understanding of what it means to be human. I realized that the apocalyptic struggle we were in, then and now, is rooted in the necessity to move toward a *true* globalization, where monotheism based on a "god out there" gives way to an interiorized spirituality rooted in the conscious union of feminine and masculine energies within and without. Where hierarchical structures are replaced by ecological structures, and where independence becomes inter-dependence. While independence speaks to establishing an identity as a separate being in the world, interdependence requires surrender to a larger sense of identity as part of the whole. Finally, it seemed imperative that we had to move from the elevation of power as strength against nature to the practice of power *with* nature and its cultural expression had to be based in Love. That is, we had to embrace a truly interdependent stance in the world based on the sacred point of origin within us.

In the late '70s, it was not uncommon to talk about the "transition" period we were in as a culture. Looking at everything from an evolutionary viewpoint, I became awed by the *magnitude* of the transition that was (is) taking place. We are in a transition as great as the transition between the matriarchal and patriarchal paradigms approximately 6,000 years ago. Although all paradigms overlap, I saw much of what was happening in the current culture as an attempt to move into this third paradigm. The numinous somatic energy that had fueled the '60s found expression in the '70's in more focused move-ments such as the human potential movement, feminism, ecology, human rights, and Eastern spirituality. During the early '80s, I frequently lectured on the transition that had to take place in us and its implications for our religious, political, and cultural institutions, particularly as we were moving into a global community. The study and reflection I did in 1980 became a platform from which I followed the emergence of a sacred, interdependent world over the next 38 years. Along with the outer events of my life, my dreams and visions, the breakthrough to the objective psyche and my attempt to understand my experience as the ongoing incarnation of Self were part of the background, the raw material, I brought into my analysis with Marion and to our friendship. What my intuitive mind envisioned needed to find resonance in my dreams and in my body. I was led to the person who could receive my experience and my longing—and all my imperfections as well.

31

As Marion was getting to know me, I was getting to know her through her writings. In her first three books I followed her journey into the wound of anorexia through to its spiritual roots and her own experience of the hidden depths of creation. Early in her life she writes about taking a piece of paper and drawing a "necklace" with several cameos in which she recorded each experience in her life where the timeless intersected time.

Perhaps one of the most memorable of these encounters with the Self she spoke of on several occasions. Following a car accident, Marion was nearly driven crazy by tinnitus, a constant ringing in the ears that was so bad at times she could barely stand it. Forced to a place of deep surrender, tinnitus would be her opening to Sophia. Exploring this event and its importance in forming her orientation towards life, she would laugh, saying "when you have a dream and a voice asks you 'how does it feel on the eve of becoming everything you've fought against all your life?' you pay attention." This statement totally puzzled her, but the answer presented itself in a vision that immediately followed the dream. Marion was filled with the scent of orange blossoms and experienced a deep love as the scent emanating out of the ground moved up her legs, penetrating each cell as it progressed. As her body surrendered, this love totally engulfed her. She was healed from the tinnitus, but more importantly by surrendering to that love, she became the orange bush, she became the perfume. In this deep surrender of the body, Marion recognized the feminine for the first time. The ego was no longer in control. In becoming one with the orange bush, the perfume, Marion experienced becoming one with the Divine beyond anything she could have imagined.

While visions often come in daytime and dreams arise from the night, they both arrive from the same source within and carry the same numinous power. Having recently become submerged in the reality of the dreamtime, I was awed by one of Marion's dreams she recorded in *The Pregnant Virgin*, although I waited until we were friends to talk about it. Several years had passed since her trip to India in 1968 but, as those who have read her account of that time know, it became another major turning point in her life, one that she continued to process until ten years later, when it culminated in a dream. In Marion's dream, a woman, wearing a peach chiffon dress and veil, is standing barefoot on the desert sand. It is noon. This numinous image is followed by the appearance of an ancient astrological clock sitting horizontally over a large wooden frame with an axle that goes deep into the earth. It is comprised of two great wheels. This is an accurate depiction of such ancient clocks, but in this case one is red and gold and the other blue and silver—acknowledging both the worldly and transcendent nature of the masculine and feminine energies. The red one turns clockwise while the blue wheel turns counter-clockwise. The wheels face the heavens while the zodiac is mirrored in the sand below. Green foliage is growing in each wheel. The whole setting of the dream speaks to a cosmic process.

The dreamer has a lover who takes his place beside the red wheel while she takes her place beside the blue one. The wheels have sharp knives radiating from the central axle and the woman's task is to dance until the wheels move synchronistically. Natives encircle the wheels and begin chanting from a deeply embodied, instinctual place. As the music begins, the woman starts to dance. Open and surrendered, she loses her fear and her body becomes a living chalice in harmony with the navel of the world, around which the wheels move. The dreamer is being danced. Representing all the energies of the psyche, the natives with one voice shift key and their music fills the heavens, at one with the music of the spheres. Green shoots and a fountain spring up in the Zodiac's third house. As we discussed this dream, I remember Marion's voice becoming deeply resonant, particularly as she tells of stopping in front of the man who "takes off my veil and says, 'Now I know your name.'"

Archetypal dreams with their vivid images come from beyond time as a gift to all of us. Each time we study them they reveal new wisdom. Sinking into these images, feeling them in my body, now that I have a deeper understanding of sound and resonance, of the connections between instinctual wisdom and the rhythm of creation, and the integration of feminine and masculine energies, the richer

Marion's dream becomes even richer for me. When we are free from the fear of the blades and spokes, the unresolved trauma in the body, the ego can resonate with a deeper vibration within, the Self/Sophia, allowing the energy to flow freely.

To lean into the wisdom of this dream is, I believe, to understand the core of Marion's life and work. Beyond the narrow confines of the temporal world, our encounters with Self/Sophia guide us in bringing the inner and outer worlds into harmony where "the dancer becomes the dance." To dance at the still point we must shift between the personal realm and the timeless transpersonal realm. More than that, we must live, surrendered to the conscious interaction of both realms taking place in us. Marion and I agreed that this dream was her pivotal encounter with the dynamic of the Self, the meeting place that she describes as a vacuum where the personal, temporal realm touches the eternal.

Arriving at the still point is to realize that one has pierced through, however briefly, to the point of origin; the pivotal, threshold place where the great unknown Reality bursts forth into time and space. It is the moment of incarnation that has been going on for billions of years; the dynamic Reality at the core of our being that wants to know It-self through us. Individually, such moments are like glimpsing the Grail knowing completion will only come with death, when we can fully embrace our true name. Yet the intensity of such experiences brings in its wake a complete reversal of how we look at ourselves, at others, and at the world. It is to enter into the flow of incarnation where one's personal psychology becomes one with the greater rhythms of creation. Meeting at this time in our lives, our shared experience and commitment to this greater Reality was the ground of our friendship.

As I was exploring my experiences of the objective psyche and its incarnation in a journal called "The Wisdom Option," (1980) Marion brought her experience to light in her books, particularly *Addiction to*

Perfection (1982). In the early 1960s, I spent two years in the California desert in complete solitude learning to meditate, while studying and writing under the weekly guidance of a spiritual director. It is in solitude that the demons, the undigested chaos within yourself, arise; but it is also a place of numinosity. Marion's "desert" was the teeming and chaotic streets of India that opened her to her unlived life.

By 1980, a common theme that emerged for both of us was a deeper realization of the oppression of the feminine within patriarchal structures. Pursuing my evolutionary approach, I remember one day really "getting it." Rage welled up within me, the rage of millions of young girls, mothers, and grandmothers over the centuries. But rage is something you need to harness in the pursuit of creative solutions within and without. At the same time, Marion was having her own negative reaction to patriarchy. As Marion delved into eating disorders, including her own, in *The Owl was a Baker's Daughter,* she began to realize the oppressive, dismissive structures in which many women have lived. The unrealized potential of women and girls, buried under an unconscious rage, was often directed toward their bodies. Even when women aligned themselves with the patriarchal power structures, they remained its victims. Feminine consciousness was lost. Digging deeper into the repressed layers of our psyche, by 1980, Marion saw that a new understanding of feminine consciousness in both women and men had to be realized if we were going to survive as a species.

Having responded to the call to reclaim the potential for a conscious interdependence, an interiorized sacred core within, and the compassion necessary for life to flourish, it became part of the dance between us. Marion recognized early on that patriarchy is "mother-bound." Born out of the repression of women and nature, it produces an immature, adolescent masculinity. Watching snippets of the 2016 Republican Primary Presidential debates, immature masculinity hits you in the face and, of course, they are mainly against women's health, environmental protection, and any measure that would truly lift up the poor. Trickle-down economics, an outdated remnant of hierarchical structures, makes interdependence or win/win scenarios impossible. I can only wonder what Marion would think of today's politically accelerated tension between progressive and regressive forces surfacing in the world at this time. We were always attuned to the culture. Clearly the necessary work to bring a mature feminine and masculine consciousness into our culture is far from over.

While Marion and I met at the still point we had each been journeying toward it for a lifetime. As she often mentioned, Marion was a minister's daughter growing up in a parsonage surrounded by the rituals of birth, marriage, and death. By the age of three she understood that the church was God's house and so she would go inside and sit very still, waiting for Him to come. The creaks and groans of the old church were surely his footsteps even if He was invisible. She also told the story of sitting on the counter looking out the kitchen window. Her father was performing a funeral in the church and three-year-old Marion was waiting for the angels to come and take the soul to heaven. From this early age her agile mind and creative imagination were attuned to the archetypal world even before she knew what that meant. This sensitivity to the invisible world led to her mother believing that something was wrong with Marion, and she often sought to remedy this "nonsense." The rejection of her natural spirituality was balanced by her father. But even with her father as an ally, the deep stirrings of her soul created an aloneness within her that set her apart from many of the pursuits and interests of her brothers and her playmates.

I had no religious upbringing beyond six Sunday mornings when a neighbor, probably fearing for my immortal soul, took me along with her children to Sunday school. I was born just three months before the beginning of World War II, so my father was away much of the time at Camp X, the secret allied intelligence training camp. My mother, a professional violinist, loved me but was more comfortable and adept cradling a violin in her arms than a child. However, within a caring extended family, I knew I was loved. Being an introvert was probably a blessing as I was happy with my books and paints, and playing with my neighborhood friends. The first real stirrings of my soul surfaced in poetry and art. At twelve, I undertook a large oil painting showing a great tree with its roots extending below the earth. Amidst its roots were the ancestors curled up in a deep sleep. At ground level a woman was stretching up the trunk of the tree, striving to reach the light that was coming from the left-hand corner above. The light illuminated the jungle-like green vegetation with large red flowers. Where that image came from in my young imagination I am not quite sure, but it did capture the intense longing I felt for a presence I could not even entertain.

Marion talked on many occasions of sleepwalking through her school years as her creative imagination did not fit in with established norms. I was an A student but dropped out of school after Grade 9. I took a secretarial course, studied art and, I will confess, spent my late afternoons in the library trying to understand Einstein! Remembering this time, the one course that Marion and I both failed was Home Economics. We often had a good laugh over that. Maybe it points to an underlying fact that given the cultural norms of 60–70 years ago, we were not destined to be very domesticated. An intense inner wildness seems to have prevailed.

Emily Dickinson became a lifeline for Marion during her teen years. The deep aloneness that comes with not being understood was alleviated as she read Emily's poetry out loud and felt it resonate within her cells. One evening, my parents thinking I was asleep, commented on the fact that they couldn't really understand me. I lay in bed, tears rolling down my cheeks because I didn't understand myself. Although I was not sure what was driving me, by the time I was 17 I found myself transplanted from Southern Ontario to Southern California. On my own and searching for meaning beyond the daily struggle that engulfed me, I began my spiritual search. Fairly early in my life, I realized that wholeness is predicated upon grasping our own uniqueness, and to achieve this requires, in most cases, a deep, necessary sense of aloneness as essential to the spiritual journey. I have certainly found this sense of aloneness to be the case in many people who, by the very nature of their longing, are forced outside the conventional norms. In analysis and workshops many women and men could relate to this reality. It led me on one occasion to give a weekend workshop entitled "Being a Unique Copy in a Xerox World."

Although Jung had many people in his life, he talked of feeling alone; the kind of aloneness that comes from knowing things other people had not experienced. Fifty years ago, I had few, if any, places to talk about the experience of the Divine Marriage, or the experience of the world beyond duality, or how to guide people to that place where the larger pattern of the dance prevails. In 1984 and 1985, boarding the subway to go to Marion's office, my soul was singing; "This woman knows, she really, really knows."

We love in the way we want to be loved, and given our complementary experiences, I believe for both Marion and me, being understood, being seen, is the primary expression of love. The spark of recognition, of deep understanding was the underlying resonance of our relationship. Nor was it by chance that we spent our lives trying to see and understand other people.

Marion often talked of seeing not only with the eyes but *through* the eyes, seeing with the inner eye of perception. Following the early Greeks, I call this seeing with immortal eyes. Sitting across from each other so many years ago, even without words, we saw and understood each other. Our individual journeys had brought us to a mutual place, a soul place capable of receiving the fullness of each other. We knew we had been given a gift, one that would unfold over the years.

THREE

The feminine learns to trust the sun before daring to move toward the moon. Psychologically, she needs to contact her own spirit and her own sense of inner order and discrimination (sun) before moving into the chaotic depths of her own body/soul (moon). Having digested these depths, she will be ready to open to the cosmos of which she is a part (stars).

Marion

Although we met at a place of deep mutuality, looking back I cannot emphasize enough the pivotal role those 49 weeks of analysis played in my ongoing journey as well as the continuing resonance that wove its way through our friendship. My analysis was truly a journey into the chaotic depths of "moon time." One of the first figures I encountered in my dreams I called Shambat after an ancient temple prostitute. Long repressed, she appeared in my dream as a huge, black woman lying on her back at the crossroads, naked, legs spread apart welcoming all comers. This same figure appeared in a second dream where we were arguing outside Marion's office. She was insisting that I bring her into the office and I was embarrassed (metaphorically and literally) to do so. Yet, this enormous embodied energy needed to be in Marion's office, the place where she could experience the love necessary for integration. During this time of my analysis, Marion was writing about the dark feminine in her dreams and the dreams of others, often appearing as a dark gypsy, or sacred prostitute, or a dancer in a tavern. If we are living a one-sided spirituality centered in the heavenly virgin, the emergence of the earthly whore is necessary to create the tension of opposites capable of transforming into the Black Madonna where the spiritual and the somatic come together.

Perhaps my embarrassment in bringing such energy into the office came through the different process Marion and I came to our conscious position. Marion was always a spiritual (religious) person, the parson's daughter. Highly intelligent and imaginative, she lived in a world of play, poetry, and scripture. The eruption in her life came through *matter*, that is through the body—through eating disorders and the great quest for perfection that led to anorexia. I had no religious upbringing. I was intelligent but moody, living in a world of art, opera, and horses. I had an Artemis streak in me and loved to ride my horse, alone in the wilderness. I had, perhaps, a more unconventional lifestyle. The eruption in my life came through *spirit* leading to a deep dedication to the spiritual life. Subsequently, having struggled for many years to maintain the "virgin place" in my psyche, by 1985 Shambat had taken on great force in my unconscious. Now, she was demanding her rightful place.

The archetypal forces of matter and spirit, feminine and masculine had to be brought into a new harmonic relationship. This balance meant opening to the energies coming up from the body and the earth and constituted the major part of my work with Marion. Having engaged my need to integrate the feminine energy, my dreams turned toward the masculine. The experience of the divine marriage mentioned above was real and life-changing, but 15 years later, I was initiated into a fuller knowledge of the bridegroom beyond the culturally determined Christian image that has distorted his true nature.

During that year with Marion, I had a series of three dreams over two weeks. In my 20's I joined the Catholic Church and this first dream came just after I had decided to leave the Church In the dream, a great raging bull came at me and when I managed to pierce it through the eye, it transformed into a black-caped devil figure. I was confronted with the culturally repressed dark side of God. A few nights later I dreamt of a great bull that came crashing out of the forest but this time it was accompanied by a shaman dressed in skins and feathers. Through ritual dancing and singing he taught me how to tame the bull. Such fierce energy should not be killed but transformed. A third dream came as I walked down into a valley where Marion was gleefully riding a horse bareback. I turned and thought I saw the bull but when I dared to come closer it was the young, dark-haired Dionysus with his goat. I made the connection to this archetypal symbol right away. When Dionysus is repressed he rages across the land like a wild bull bringing destruction in his wake. When he is honored, the energy he brings forth liberates and knocks down walls. He brings fluidity to what has become rigid. He is the god of ecstasy and the dance. No wonder he was also one of the first gods banned by Christianity. His re-entry into my conscious awareness would open me to the more instinctual layers of my psyche.

As my feminine and masculine consciousness was opening to the embrace of both realms; spirit and matter, heaven and earth, the possibility for a new union, a further transformation surfaced in a dream I had nine months into my analysis. This dream took place in moon time, the time of the goddess:

> *A full moon is shining in through the bedroom window. I am lying in bed slightly elevated and bouncing a baby on my stomach. Marion is lying on my left side and analyst Marie Louise von Franz is lying on my right. Von Franz gets up and says that we must be getting on with it. (I forget the exact words, but Marion laughed and said it sounded just like her.)*

Following the emergence of a more integrated, conscious masculine and feminine energy a totally new energy, aided by the "mother" and the "grandmother," was born out of the nine months of my analysis. The birth of this new androgynous energy within my psyche echoed Marion's dreams and writing of a few years earlier. It provided part of the creative tension each of us continued to work on individually as well as discuss and share for many years to come.

My dreams were largely archetypal and, like the dream above, some of the most important took place in moonlight, in the time of the goddess. In one dream I was sitting in the lotus position in the center of a large field under a bright full moon. In my hands I was holding a great white serpent that had come up out of the earth. It aligned itself with my body, standing straight up beyond my head. All around, as far as I could see, giant white serpents were rising straight up out of the earth. It was an awe-inspiring dream but at that time I knew nothing about white serpents. I learned that as our feminine and masculine energies become more integrated, this great life force capable of uniting earth and heaven arises not only in us but throughout the world. This is one of those lifetime dreams that I still ponder. In another dream, a full moon shone in the window awakening me from sleep. A cat (feminine instinct) jumped on the bed and led me out of the room to a descending staircase. On the second landing an ancient, "Paleolithic," young couple were gently making love.

It took me a few years beyond my analysis to understand the container that Sophia was weaving, and several more years to realize its importance for a further task she would ask of me. One Sunday in the spring of 1987, I went over to Marion's Walmer Road apartment for brunch. Immediately, she recognized my enthusiasm. "I have finally got it," I exclaimed, "it" being one of the major reasons why my analysis was so important, particularly with Marion. What precipitated this insight was a picture I came across in an Egyptian import shop depicting the judgment of Maat, the Egyptian goddess of justice. It showed a pole with seven nodules, representing the chakras standing upright, while from the crosspiece hung a scale at either end. A crocodile stood menacingly between the second and third nodule, while a bird-like god rested on the top. A person's heart was placed in one scale to be balanced against a feather from Maat's headdress in the other. Somehow that symbolic painting captured my process.

The importance of my analysis lay in the fact that the great white light that had inundated my being and left me with the feeling of being lifted up into the heavens needed to be grounded in the earth. The great white serpent energy, the transformed instinctual energy that was coming up through me was also the same energy that was being brought into consciousness throughout creation. This core symbol I would realize more profoundly many years later in my journey. For now, I realized that the white serpents coming up through the earth and aligning with my body were showing me that the energies of the first chakra and the seventh chakra had to be brought together in the heart. The next dream of the ancient couple making love in the second chakra mirrored the divine marriage taking place through the sixth chakra. In both cases, instinct and image, matter and spirit were being brought into harmony through the heart.

The third and fifth chakras are masculine chakras, that is, they have to do with communication and moving out into the world. If the third chakra becomes rigid with unchallenged ideologies or scripts learned from childhood or cultural patterns, the fifth, or voice chakra, will largely be limited to platitudes. I had thought of myself as fairly open to new ideas and experiences but I realized that a residue of negative feelings can reinforce the scripts we are barely aware of.

During my analysis, with Marion's advice, I worked on a weekly basis with John Went. Before founding the Integral Healing Centre, John worked primarily through bioenergetics, the energy processes in the body often leading to the release of unconscious emotions. Anger we are aware of, rage is unconscious. My rage was rooted in my adolescence and I remember one day finally releasing it and, in the process, throwing a large dictionary against the wall so hard it broke the binding, exploding it into three pieces. Driving back to the office that day I felt ten years younger. Interestingly, having released my rage, I noticed my clients were beginning to release their rage. Although nothing was said, obviously they felt safe. The field around us had changed.

Aware that I was propelled into analysis by my ungrounded flurry of activity ending in pleurisy and not being able to breathe, Marion felt I should do some voice work. Having worked with John in releasing the rage in my body, Marion knew a further step would be to allow the voice to arise naturally from its own instinctual depths connecting spiritual energy with deep emotion and imagination. When we can speak from this place, the truth and love behind our words becomes palpable in the environment around us.

An authentic voice, be it spoken, sung, or expressed in written language, supports a flexible mind within a resonant body. I continue to work on this but, as usual, dreams point the way. In a dream towards the end of my analysis, Marion and I find a wild, white horse that has been running in a field. Under Marion's tutelage, we take it up to the door of the convent/monastery. In the dream, the instinctual life, the passion of the body, had been tamed and was now available to me. At the same time, my dream was telling me that my embodied energy was not welcome in the convent. Changing the "outer" garments, the conscious scripts such as new works, new ways of organizing, was all that was envisioned.

In the second part of the dream, I looked through a large opening in the rocks and there in a deep, underground cavern, I discovered a large golden cathedral. The walls, everything, were bathed in gold. The priest was dressed in gold robes and held a gold chalice lifted up in the sacrifice of the Mass. I needed Marion's help to interpret that dream: This cavernous inner cathedral was bathed in congealed light, alchemical gold; the interplay between the masculine and feminine within, transcendence and immanence. The feminine chalice in the Mass constantly receives and issues forth the incarnate God of life, death, and resurrection. This exchange symbolizes the work that goes on in the center, the Self. Clearly the light now emanating from the body spoke to an interiorized spirituality, but it also became a symbol for me of the ongoing transformation of spirit into matter and matter into spirit.

In 49 hours of analysis, my inner landscape was shaped by the thoughts and language of Jung but, more importantly, by the thoughts and language of Marion. In my earlier dream I was led to Jung's office but at the heart of his office is Marion's office, firmly planted on the earth and open to the sky. While my analysis was conducted within a Jungian framework, my dream images reflect the emergence of a feminine consciousness at the core of a new dispensation. Marion, partly by virtue of being a woman, but mostly through her own experience of bringing forth the light in matter, was able to open this creative matrix to me and so many others. Continuing incarnation can only take place through a feminine consciousness open to all of nature. The dark feminine and the dark masculine energy that came in my dreams rooted me in the earth while being open to the sky. Marion not only contained and bore witness to my soul's emergence, but a further gift was to give me a *language* with which to articulate the depths and dynamics of the psyche, the connectedness of the world within and the world without. In turn, my gift to her was my ability to use that language to recognize and affirm the depths she was probing. In time, it became evident that my dreams of the dark goddess, the transformation of the masculine, the rising energies of the body and the earth and their balance in the heart was feeding into Marion's journey. From the beginning, it seems Sophia was weaving the threads that would become the tapestry of our friendship.

One of Marion's favorite quotes was from Etty Hillesum's *An Interrupted Life*. "Mysticism must rest on crystal clear honesty, can only come after things have been stripped down to their naked reality."[4] This sentence recalls an evening early on in our friendship. In 1989, I moved into a new home and Marion, bearing gifts, came for a house-warming dinner. Later, sitting in my living room, she causally threw out the idea of how difficult it is to be really, really, honest about the depths, the light and dark, of our inner life. *Yes*, I thought, *how much do we dare open ourselves to the unconscious and when we do, how much do we ever really admit to?* Whether this was a rhetorical statement or a challenge in our ongoing relationship, I was not sure. Sharing at this level only comes after we have worked diligently on our material "in secret," much like an oyster producing the pearl. To have a place of trust to bring forth our pearls, be they black or white, is invaluable. One advantage of moving from analyst

---

[4] Woodman, Marion. (2000). *Bone* (p. 43). New York, N.Y. New York: Viking Penguin.

to friend is that Marion certainly had great insight into the heights and depths of me. As a friend, I believe I came to know her almost as deeply.

That evening in June of 1989, I remember we talked about her relationship with her husband Ross, but mainly about the insights gleaned from our own inner journeys. As often happened, we were amazed at the depths we came to and the energy that flowed, needing to express our gratitude in either a phone call or a note. Following this occasion, I received a message from Marion that said: "Just received your beautiful message on my machine. Yes, it was a very special evening—a moment in time... As always, you leave me with something meaty to think about. It is so validating to talk to you. Thank you, Elinor. Thank you for being such an understanding, sensitive friend." Those sentiments were certainly shared.

PART II

REFLECTIONS ON OUR INTERPERSONAL DANCE

FOUR

Feminine consciousness finds what is meaningful to it and plays. It may work very hard, but its attitude is always one of play because it loves life.

Marion

The springtime of our relationship carried with it great energy and joy. Our souls resonated on many levels. At one level we found our Scottish roots. Although Marion's father had been here for some generations, and mine arrived as a young man, they came from the same part of Scotland. My father had no religious affiliation while Marion's father was a United Church minister. Yet both our fathers were Freemasons, and both could quote Robbie Burns poetry at any given moment. We even shared a good Scottish middle name, Jean. Perhaps, important in any relationship, we appreciated each other's sense of humor—usually served dry with a keen sense of the absurd. I never thought much of our Scottish roots, but they came to the surface one day in August of 2014. The Queen was going to open the Commonwealth Games in Scotland and I suggested we turn on the television to watch. Marion became bored, so we turned off the television and, sitting back, proceeded to sing in our best Scottish accent all the old songs we knew so well: "Roamin' in the Gloamin,'" "Loch Lomond," and "I Belong to Glasgow." It brought back memories of the two of us walking along St. Clair one evening in the falling snow singing Christmas carols. While the soul loves to make a joyous sound, given our singing voices at this time, I did get up and close the door.

While opposites do attract, as Jung pointed out, beneath the personal unconscious there are deep ancestral patterns belonging to a region or culture that the psyche resonates with, providing a natural level of understanding and familiarity. Looking back, I think that was part of the ease between us throughout our friendship.

Family was often part of our ongoing conversation going back to the early days of our friendship. "Have you ever wanted children?" Marion asked. "I've never had an overwhelming desire," I replied. "It's probably just as well since I never married." "I ached to have a child," she whispered, "but my lengthy battle with anorexia made it impossible. I never practiced birth control because I knew I couldn't get pregnant." It was August of 1987, and we were lying on the warm, ancient rocks of her summer home overlooking Georgian Bay. I heard the longing and grief in Marion's voice. After a few minutes of silence, I turned my head to look at her and said, "But in many ways, I believe we attended a lot of births." She smiled.

Apart from a shared heritage, we discovered many other levels of interest reflected in the books that lined the shelves of our somewhat large and eclectic libraries. Among them were books by Jung, von Franz, and other Jungians, as well as books on science. (In 1979 we had both read Gary Zukav's *The Dancing Wu Li Masters,* one of the first books to articulate the dynamic of fields and the integration of quantum physics and Jung.) There were also books by Thomas Merton, Juliana of Norwich, Teresa d'Avila, Teilhard de Chardin, Lao Tse, Thomas Berry, and many others. As we both had degrees in English literature, our shared interests included many of the same novelists and poets, including Blake, Shelley, Yeats, and T. S. Eliot. One evening at dinner, for some reason I started quoting from Tennyson's "Ulysses": "I am a part of all that I have met..." Marion joined in and we finished the long poem together.

Theatre had been a great love in each of our lives. Yellowed programs posted in an old scrapbook list Marion's little theatre performances in plays by George Bernard Shaw and many others. After teaching for one year, in 1952 Marion went off to London,

England, to secretly pursue a career on the stage. I was told she made an impression, not only with her acting but with her comedic ability, being hailed as the next Margaret Rutherford. In spite of her success, a combination of factors, including disapproval from her family, led to her return to London, Ontario. I caught a glimpse of her ability during a 2014 Christmas gathering in London with Ann and Wendy. In response to Ann's question of what she might like to do next with her life, Marion mischievously replied that she thought she would return to the stage. Knowing her history, Ann took up the playful pulse of the moment mentioning some roles from various plays such as *The Importance of Being Ernest*. Immediately Marion got into character, and with arms outstretched she began to give a robust rendition of her lines. I was quite astounded. The playful passion of her soul was on full display.

In 1953, Marion returned to South Secondary School in London, Ontario. Here she taught English Literature using her prodigious knowledge of literature and her dramatic ability. Teaching high school English allowed her to express her creativity to the benefit of the many students she taught over 23 years. Music, art, drama, and literature came alive for her students through the Creative Arts program she established. It was during this time Marion became aware of the trans-formative effect that reading in dramatic form had on adolescents.

During my university days in the mid- to late '60s, I delighted in directing plays. While Marion presented Blake's poem "Heaven and Hell" performed by a voice choir, I remember using imagery and voice choirs to present the work of T. S. Eliot, and on one Christmas, a rendition of the long word poem, *A Woman Wrapped in Silence*. While I appreciated Shakespeare, I was drawn toward what I called "musicals with meaning." My most successful "in house" production was a full-length play based on an adaptation of Winnie-the-Pooh. The cast and I were reduced to hysterical laughter throughout rehearsals as Kanga, Roo, Tigger, Winnie, and Eeyore, evoked the psychological types of the actors I had picked to play them.

While Marion and Ross performed Nagg and Nell in Beckett's *Endgame*, my stage presence was limited to the Saturday-night campus pub crowd. Using the head of a large industrial mop for a wig and appropriately clothed for the '60s flower-power generation, I did a one-woman show strumming on a guitar and reciting Leonard Cohen-style word poems I had written. These offerings were satirical and hopefully, insightful, renditions of the lives of many of my friends in the audience. Inscribed on a roll of toilet paper the "poetry" could be torn off and distributed among them to use as they wished.

Although we didn't know each other in our younger years, we discovered that we shared many interests. By my mid-forties I had become quite serious, but my earlier sense of creative, often irreverent, playfulness was restored in my relationship with Marion. However, it was our passion for the inner life that generated the great enthusiasm that intuitive people share when uncovering new insights. Finding, or perhaps losing, ourselves in the archetypal, timeless realm, we often remarked how the hours seemed to fly. I called it "playing in the land of three times ten."

One Christmas in the early '90s, we had brunch at Marion's place before she went to London. I arrived around 10:30 a.m. and we ate and shared our latest adventures and insights. After a time, I looked at my watch. It was 1:00 p.m. The vice president of St. Michaels Hospital was having a Christmas party for department heads from 4:00 to 7:00 p.m. that day. Lots of time! We watched the latest hour-long video in the Bly and Woodman series, made another cup of tea and discussed many, many things. Suddenly, we realized it was dark. I looked at my watch again. It was 8:30 p.m.!! We just looked at each other and started to laugh. Once again, we were amazed at the intensity of our encounter.

During the years following my analysis, I would take the subway up to Marion's office on St. Clair, picking up Swiss Chalet for dinner. Orders were placed on whether we were feeling good or bad—the former meant salad and the latter meant French fries with our chicken breast. Of course, it was all soul food! One evening I arrived with a Peanuts cartoon strip. As I remember it from 30 years ago, Lucy and Charlie Brown were lying on the side of a hill looking up at the clouds. Charlie Brown asked Lucy what images she saw in the clouds. Lucy gave her typical reply: "I see a castle and a moat with a drawbridge and knights riding out on grey chargers with flying banners of purple, gold, and red. What do you see, Charlie Brown?" "Well, I was going to say I saw a doggie and a ball." Turning to Marion I commented, "That is the difference between you and me—Lucy." It is the difference between my inferior thinking function and Marion's inferior sensation function. Because our inferior function is closest to the unconscious, dreams, and at the deepest level, our imagination, comes through that function. I can have detailed dreams, but they usually have an easily recognizable logical structure. Marion's dreams carry the artistic detail of all the senses.

Close relationships often develop their own unique patterns of interacting. This was true of Marion and me. In November 2014, I first told Marion about the dream telling me to write about our friendship, and I read to her the first few pages of this manuscript. When I read the paragraph describing the still point (p.30) she gave me the "arched eyebrow." "Did you write that!" meaning, of course, it was very good. In return I gave her my snarly "curled lip" response. It brings a smile to my heart remembering how often we had such exchanges over the years.

We both had busy schedules in the mid-1980s and '90s, but we managed to make time to talk and play, a pattern which lasted for the next 15 years. One Friday afternoon, probably in the early '90s, Marion had just gotten into Toronto as she had a weekend workshop with the poet David Whyte. She needed a ride to the hotel at Highway 401 and Yorkdale Drive. I was happy to oblige and remained for the weekend. Saturday morning, Marion was talking and said something about her dear friend, pointing to me in the front row. There were about 150-200 people attending, many from the States. I became somewhat of a curiosity! Around 5 p.m. on Sunday, when the workshop was finished, I drove Marion back to her apartment at Walmer Road. We were both too tired to go out, and because Marion hadn't been in Toronto all week, a ripe banana and two slightly stale muffins would be our supper. With great flourish, Marion got out her linen tablecloth, best dishes, crystal, and china teacups. There was always plenty of good English tea. While we were reviving the muffins in the microwave and making tea, I told her about people wanting to know if I was really Marion's friend. "I hope you said yes," she responded.

Perhaps inspired by the last two days I started to dance around the apartment and spontaneously began to sing:

> The question is posed, are you Marion's friend?
> I smile demurely, with a simple "yes."
> Can they even guess the smile within
> the joyous, shimmering, reverent depths
> from which that "yes" resounds.

Laughing, Marion tossed my muffin at me. "But really!" I could only say, "What do you expect when you drag me to a poetry workshop!"

One evening Marion recalled one of our adventures to Ann and Wendy. She remembered our going to the Royal Alexander Theatre to see Lily Tomlin in her remarkable one-woman show *The Search for Signs of Intelligent Life in the Universe.* With great humor and cutting insight, Trudy, the Times Square bag lady and philosopher, had the audience in the palm of her hand. After two hilarious and insightful hours we were compelled to go out on the town to celebrate, an excursion Marion emphasized by remarking to Wendy and Ann, "I don't live a flat life, you know."

Marion playing the role of a bag lady.

(I saw this photo at Marion's one day, and when she asked me what I would like for Christmas, I pointed to the picture. She laughed, as apparently Ross had the same request. We each received a copy in a beautiful, bleached-wood frame. The story that goes with the picture is that Marion was in costume on the street when a very kind lady came up to fix her disheveled clothing. Marion decided to stay in character, respectfully honoring the love and concern.)

FIVE

It is at the place of wounding that we find ourselves connected to each other in love.

Marion

Shared vulnerability is the foundation stone of an enduring relationship.

Elinor

When a relationship is taken outside the container of analysis there is a risk that new, unconscious material will surface. The first months following my analysis our friendship contained great joy and some anguish. It is difficult to remember specifics now, but I recall my inner struggles as to whether this woman was as realized as I thought her to be or whether I had a projection after all. In terms of our relationship, she seemed to alternatively "blow hot or cold." There were days when I fought with myself trying to reach a decision whether or not to forego our relationship altogether. Amidst the great energy and joy of our times together there were times when I was taken aback. There were occasions when we had an absolutely wonderful time and then at the very end she would come out with a zinger that hit me like an arrow, or I would be invited over for dinner to find she wasn't there; apparently out buying wallpaper for her living room. This happened on another occasion but there was one particular incident that led to a complete breakdown and things erupted. Marion had phoned from London asking me to get theatre tickets on such-and-such a date but on the evening in question, when I went to pick her up no one was home. I was disappointed, but I was also angry. I knew enough to realize my reaction was my problem and it was my decision as to whether I could deal with this inconsistency, without understanding what it meant. Having to be self-sufficient from a very young age, I had developed a fine, but steel-like, filter around my heart that allowed me to withdraw from any seemingly negative situation or relationship quickly and easily. Yet here was a person with so much integrity and insight who had become so important to me that, from my point of view, it was a relationship worth fighting for.

Not wanting to let the sun set on my anger I drove up to the Jung Foundation offices later that evening and waited as I knew Marion was attending a meeting. Apart from being conflicted, I felt rather foolish and undignified. Later Marion would comment how relieved she was to walk out and see me there. Things were talked out that night. I expressed how confused I was by her conflicting behavior. Marion thought, perhaps, she just didn't have time for a close friend. Very lovingly, I replied that felt like BS—the easy way out. At this stage of our lives there were few projections or expectations in our relationships. Since we were both capable of "kissing the joy as it flies," I knew there was something deeper that was operating both in Marion and in me. Marion realized that unconsciously, she was doing the same thing she had done with her analyst, Dr. Bennett, some years before; sabotaging her appointment by showing up on the wrong day and then feeling rejected. Such "mistakes" were unusual because she was committed to her process and generally prompt and on time for any meeting. Dr. Bennett realized she was unconsciously writing down the times incorrectly therefore setting up an antagonistic situation with him. The real dynamic, as Dr. Bennett pointed out, was fear in the face of anyone who truly loved her, and subsequently setting up a way to get out of the relationship. She had to admit she couldn't take the risk of being abandoned.

Many years had passed since Marion had brought the fear of abandonment to consciousness and, like many of us in similar situations she thought she was "done with that." But that night in 1987 we both discovered in different ways, that our friendship, rooted as it was in the archetypal depths, had become so meaningful, that deep issues around trust, of the old, unconscious fear of abandonment rooted in the cells of the body surfaced once more. For me, I had to admit that the finely woven wall around my heart was equally challenged. Through the depth of our relationship, each in our own way had touched our deepest fear. This would not have happened in an analytic or workshop situation where the container held trust in a more prescribed manner. We agreed that the container between us had to be in real time for further growth to occur. The emphasis, of course, is on growth and growth implies, in Marion's words, an increasing ability to enter into the irrational space of our own darkness and trusting the other in that darkness.

Trust is the cornerstone of love and unconditional love cannot exist without unconditional trust. This is not an ideal that the ego can commit itself to; it is not an agreed-upon set of conditions that we, consciously or unconsciously, wrap our expectations of the other around. *Unconditional* love and *unconditional* trust can only come through surrender to something greater than us; in our case, surrender to Sophia's choreography as it unfolds between two. Reaffirming our relationship as an unfolding of Sophia's dance is reflected in Marion's words: "Real love happens when embodied soul meets embodied soul. Not in spirit, not in that disembodied world where we want to be perfect, but in life ... when we're doing things we didn't think we could do, when we're stripped of all pride. Our friend is stripped; we are stripped. There is no false modesty. We are stripped of everything that is unreal and the two of us are there together. I can't even put it into words. Where soul meets soul, that's love."[5]

When visiting Marion in the summer of 2014, she turned to me with considerable anxiety and said, "You will continue to visit me,

---

[5] Woodman, Marion. (1993). *Conscious Femininity* (pp. 88-89). Toronto, Ontario: Inner City Books.

Elinor?" I felt this urgent question was spoken against what the future might bring. I assured her that went without saying. Later, walking down the hall she squeezed my hand. Looking straight ahead, she said, "When you're here I know who I am." For over 30 years we had been "home" to each other and a mirror for each other. In old age nothing had changed. Intimacy, rooted in Sophia, kept the mirror clear.

When someone asked Dr. von Franz what psychological types would have the greatest difficulty trusting each other, her response garnered some surprise. She said the two types that would have the greatest difficulty are introverted feelers with extraverted intuition and extraverted feelers with introverted intuition. That is, two strong intuitive feelers with their intense energy going in opposite directions will have difficulty trusting each other. Great energy coupled with extraverted feeling can appear to arise from ego, while introverted feeling can appear as aloof or uninvolved. While I never experienced an excess of ego in Marion, sometimes her energy can seem overly confident or overwhelming. My natural contemplative nature irked her when I slipped into passivity. At such times we had the inner freedom to call each other out if necessary. When a response for some irritation was called for, the direct, flat-footed approach seemed most economical. Luckily, each of us could hold the tension and the intensity with which we lived our lives in our own way, and that basic sense of self-acceptance extended into our relationship. We could be lovingly direct with each other, so going forward, trust was never a problem.

Of course, the shadow lives on—always. We certainly knew each other's shadow but it was no longer a cause for distrust; at best it occasioned a raised eyebrow. When it comes to shadow stuff, my unconscious doesn't let me get away with a thing. I remember one night making an uncalled for critical statement to Marion on the phone. I woke up the next morning with a dream that made me both groan—and laugh. We were in a mansion and Marion was showing me a large, precious jewel. While the mansion and jewel are symbols of our relationship, in the dream there was a man, intoxicated and bumping into everything. On the previous evening this was clearly my animus, not dangerous but obnoxious and totally out of line. I quickly phoned Marion to apologize. Similarly, one day at a conference at New College we were going into lunch when Marion came out with a first-class patriarchal statement that made my head spin. Early the next morning the phone rang with "You must have thought I fell into....." In both cases we knew there was no conscious intention to hurt and so it was easy to let go and even laugh. Perfection is not an option; being responsible for our imperfection is the best we can do.

SIX

To be aware of one's own feelings, needs, and values and to have the courage to act on them, is the essence of conscious femininity.

Marion

While we are ultimately responsible for our own decisions, deep friendship offers us a safe, loving space in which to explore our options. In turn, this witnessing gives us the ability to listen to ourselves and our body's response. Over the years we have alternatively played that role for each other. Certainly, Marion contained and witnessed me during the year of my analysis while I contained and witnessed her during the years of illness and when her work was challenged. Such witnessing was a spontaneous, consistent pattern throughout our friendship.

One space we held for each other was around our relationships. Shortly after finishing my analysis in 1985, I was driving Marion home from her office when she said, "Would you like to come up to the island in August? Besides having time to spend together, I have told Ross all about you and he is eager to meet you." Sha Sha, a large magical island in Georgian Bay, pulsates with archetypal energy that is both challenging and healing. While our week together was filled with memories, my welcome that first evening still makes my heart smile. In the rugged wilderness of the Precambrian Shield, Ross had built an authentic Japanese tea house. I was to be the first official guest, so after sunset we made our way there. I settled in letting go of city stress while Marion massaged my feet with oil, an ancient custom of greeting to be sure, and Ross read a short story by Alice Munro. The next thing I remember is waking up with the sun streaming through the large window. My dreams bore witness to the fact that my body/soul had been truly fed.

The week went by quickly. Ross swam in the morning while Marion and I swam or bathed in the afternoon before preparing supper. One day during a picnic lunch, we discovered that I had met Ross even before I met Marion. That is, in 1968 I had based one of my major English papers at the University of Toronto on Ross's book *The Apocalyptic Vision in the Poetry of Shelley.* Most days we took some time to work on our individual projects that, in turn, we shared after dinner. It was during this time that Marion wrote her short story, "The Man She Never Married." Our conversations were rich and lively. Other times we just read poetry aloud or said prayers while we watched the sun set. As Marion and I explored the island, conversation and the deep silence of nature became equal beats of our rhythm.

Marion always spoke of Ross's ability to gently probe and listen to people, inviting them to share their life's story. After a few days of getting to know me, Ross sat back and quoted the poet Blake, "Improvement makes straight roads; but the crooked roads without Improvement are roads of Genius."[6] I laughed. For me, our Genius is an aspect of soul that remembers our pattern before we were born and continues to guide our destiny. That being the case, my Genius never did take the straight roads that our culture lays out to guide and improve us. Between leaving home at 17 with very little money and a Grade Nine education and where I was today, involved some circuitous, one might even say miraculous, routes.

---

[6] Blake, William. (1958). *Blake Poems and Letters* (p. 98). In J. Bronowski (Ed.). New York, New York: Penguin Books.

The day I left Sha Sha was Marion's birthday and that morning Ross presented us both with poems. My poem was inspired by the fact that before coming to the island I had officially received my papers from the Vatican releasing me from my vows. The poem told of Marion and me on the island and ended with the image of "the high priestess raising her chalice, coming home to herself at last."

Pictures taken at Sha Sha, 1986.

In the fall of that same year, Marion and I went down to London to attend a day-long seminar on neurobiology at Western University. We stayed at Wharncliffe Road, the house she and Ross had lived in since they were married 25 years before. Ross happened to be away. Upon arrival, Marion gave me a tour, which was like going through an art gallery. Three floors of rooms were filled with paintings and sculptures, including the bathrooms! As well as being a notable Professor of Romantic Literature, Ross was an art collector of some stature. As we moved through the house, Marion kept repeating, "You see, there is no room for me here. He fills all the space!" I understood her frustration and the ambivalent message she was receiving. On the other hand, Ross, I thought was, at least partially, filling the space because of Marion's absence! At the very least they were each following their passion. To follow one's passion, to follow one's Genius, requires a strong, flexible container, particularly in a marriage. These were the spaces Marion and Ross had to create in their relationship. Over the years, they often talked about the many marriages they went through in exploring the challenge of creating those spaces. Many of their insights were shared with the world in writing, in storytelling and in film. One breakthrough in their marriage came as Marion and I were writing *Dancing in the Flames.* While the three of us were sitting in the garden having tea, Ross recounted that unexpected moment when all the projections fell away, and he experienced his wife as a complete stranger. Given to "crystal clear honesty in relationship," they decided that this insight had to be included in our book. Overall, the depth and honesty of the process they articulated is a legacy for anyone who wants to delve more deeply into the role of marriage in the individuation process.

To work out the individuation process through a marriage can be a lifetime task. While the inner marriage is not unrelated to the outer marriage, it has a life of its own. I confess, what garnered my enthusiasm, and what Marion and I talked about a lot, was the inner marriage. Collectively, to evolve to a new level of consciousness will require a new understanding of who we are as humans. We must go beyond our present stereotypes based on gender. The biological, psychological and spiritual levels of our being need to be integrated within and without. The pulse of life experienced as Love, requires the integration of both masculine and feminine energies in both women and men. It is the integration of these two energies that must be present in our perception of, and action in, the world.

At the end of *The Ravaged Bridegroom*, Marion writes: "Our responsibility is to the present, to the images that guide us, to the two energies that together are love."[7] The image she gives us for this

---

[7] Woodman, Marion. (1990). *The Ravaged Bridegroom* (pp. 216-217). Toronto, Ontario: Inner City Books.

integrated energy is that of the dreamer and her beloved as partners in a creativity contest. They are building a boat and are trying to think of what to use as a sail.

> We talk and kiss each other and try to think of a sail. I lie in the boat with my head by the mast. Suddenly, I've got it. So has he. He kneels beside me and weaves my long blond hair into a golden sail. A quick gust fills it. My beloved grabs the rudder and we are carried out into a sunlit sea. I don't know if we win the contest. Nothing matters except that I love him and he loves me and we both love the water and the wind. I am the sail, he is the rudder. In our little craft we are borne by the Holy Spirit over the eternal sea.[8]

While the feminine catches the spirit that propels the process, the masculine holds the container steady.

With women, the tale of Psyche and Aphrodite is a great starting point for the work of feminine and masculine integration. To reclaim the true beauty at the core of her being and bring that beauty into the world, Psyche must first learn to surrender to the goddess who initiates her into the work of integrating her inner masculine, a mature Eros, capable of carrying love and beauty out into the world.

The larger story in which the tale of Psyche is embedded, *The Golden Ass of Apuleius*, is a similar guide to the differentiation of the feminine in man and his meeting with the great goddess Isis who leads him to his true self. One evening, I was talking on the phone with a former client about some wonderful things that were happening in his life. Early the next morning I received a phone call saying that he was dead. A heart attack! Thoughtfully, a dream was delivered to me that he had recorded that morning. He was standing at the edge of a river when he noticed a numinous female figure coming toward him. She led him across a "rainbow" bridge. He had done deep work on the Mother Complex and how that had affected his relationships with

---

[8] Ibid., p. 217.

women. At 60, he died relatively young, and at a memorial for him I read the words of Sophia: "But the just man, though he die early, shall be at rest. For the age that is honorable comes not with the passing of time, nor can it be measured in terms of years." (Wisdom 4: 7-8). A long life is not as important as the degree of consciousness you attain. As you might imagine, these were themes Marion and I talked about on more than one occasion.

One evening in the mid-'90s, Marion remarked that she had become aware of two men currently circling in my orbit. She was particularly fond of one and pressed me on where I thought the relationship might go. "We are friends," I said, but I felt both men wanted more. Although I enjoyed their company, my reluctance to make a further commitment was obvious. Laughing, she said, "Well, it's not like you have to get married!"

Marion was well aware of an old tension in me going back many years. Coming from a small General Motors town, by my mid-teens, I was aware that my expected future lay in getting married, living in the suburbs with two children and two cars in the driveway. I was paralyzed by the thought: the circumscribed inevitability of my life. In 1956, it motivated my flight to California. Of course, the cultural scripts of the time, not to say hormones, remained strong and at 19 I got engaged. At the same time, I became immersed in the books of Thomas Merton, the first of my "Three Wise Men." (Thomas Berry and Carl Jung were the other two men who deeply influenced my life. All, I realize now, were scholars and mystics.) Merton introduced me to the spiritual quest, the life of solitude and contemplation. My passion went in that direction. Although I paid little attention to dogma, in 1959, I became a Catholic lured by the deep spiritual tradition. My engagement to the young Navy Lieutenant ended when I made the decision to go into solitude in the California desert for two years. Having returned to Canada, four years later, a second engagement ended with my entering the convent. In the underlying tension between the demands of convention and biology, and the call to follow where the spirit led, it was the latter that won out. While I could distinguish between the inner and outer lover, I could never reconcile the demands that each placed on me. The inner always had much more pull, and I ended up hurting the men in question. Such was the basis for my current reluctance.

I have often thought if I was meant to achieve my destiny, or aspects of my individuation through relationship with the outer lover, I would have met someone earlier who could hold the intensity of my passion for the inner life and had the desire to grow with me.

While Marion and Ross talked about their many "marriages," I realized that as with a dedicated relationship in real life, in our psychic life we can also go through many "marriages" as we continue to grow. As mentioned earlier, in 1970, after much anguish I surrendered to an invitation to the divine marriage. By 1976, another defining vision took the gift of that marriage through a further spiral. While sitting in a large, crowded chapel, I became aware of an enormous Christ figure kneeling in the sanctuary. He had his back to me as He prayed. He was clothed in a long, red robe. Slowly He turned and came toward me taking the crown of thorns from His own head and placing it on mine. Tears started to roll down my face. Six years before I was terrified of what my surrender to the Beloved would mean. Now, with greater understanding, I was able to feel joy at the prospect that I would not only love but be able to love completely; at least before I die! While keenly aware of my weakness, to love completely, to become love, was my overriding desire. To receive the martyr's crown is the opposite of being victim. It is the martyr who knows that love is stronger than death; a knowledge that would be tested in the years to come. The ability to surrender to a greater level of reality that includes life and death, and, indeed, all the opposites, was taking shape. Our union reached a new level of maturity.

A third spiral of love necessitated my need for the container of analysis with Marion as the culturally outcast aspects of the Beloved had to be realized through the integration of the repressed Dionysian energy. While my encounter with the Christ energy opened me up to the possibilities of love, it was only when I left the confines of The Church that the repressed, embodied energy made its appearance. It took the ancient shaman in my dreams to teach me how to transform the deadly Demon Lover into the earthy, ecstatic Dionysus (pp. 37-38). Connected to the earth and the feminine, Dionysus was (is) the energy suppressed by the Church and so was left unconscious to wander with his wanton ways. This ongoing integration of my masculine energy eventually led to a deeper understanding of *embodied* spirituality; the incarnate experience of life, death, and rebirth. In turn, my understanding of Sophia as a symbol of the Self was greatly expanded. For Sophia to fully operate in the world as Creative Wisdom, both an articulated and integrated feminine and masculine energy must be present.

As Sophia doesn't miss an opportunity to instruct us, in 1987 a theologian friend sent me a thesis by Elizabeth Johnson published in the *Ephemerides Theologieae Lavanienses 61*. The major theme of Johnson's work centered on Christ as the Incarnation of Sophia. The words of love and inclusion that Christ speaks in the Gospel are the words of Sophia taken from the Wisdom literature of the Old Testament. It is Sophia/Christ that goes into the marketplace inviting everyone to partake of the banquet. While She can chastise, the words spoken are words of love. Just as Eros symbolizes the outward expression of Aphrodite's love, on another level, Christ symbolizes the outward expression of Sophia's love, the creative force that binds all worlds together. I was not only being called to love but I was beginning to understand the masculine energy that would carry that love out into the world. Christ/Sophia became the personification of the integrated divine energy in the core of my B/being just as it did for Marion. As a dedication in the beginning of *Bones*, Marion wrote; *"To my still point that is Sophia and Christ."*

Our conversation on that particular evening in the mid-'90's turned to Ross writing a poem for her every year on her birthday. "It was one way," Marion laughed, "to keep track of the pulse of our relationship." Jokingly I said, "Well, I won't be receiving any poems from my lover." The next morning, I awoke with a poem in my head so clear that I managed to write it down.

> My lover writes no poems for me,
> His crowning gift a thorn
> that pierced my flesh, my heart, my soul,
> Love's seed there to be sown.

With gentle eyes, caressing thighs
He filled me with His light
and shattered all the boundaries
that I once knew as life.
With blazing eyes, hands of ice
He held me in death's vice
and stripped from me all surety
that I once grasped as life.
Surrendered, prostrate, opening up
desire transfixed on pyre,
consumed in mists of mystery,
the lotus heart on fire.
We danced across the dew of dawn
far into darkest night.
Ah, well I know the edge between
the darkness and the light.

At times the unconscious can be playful and equally precise in the images it presents. This night-time poem felt like an affirmation that I made the right decision many years ago.

While women often entertain the masculine energy, inner or outer, during our friendship many other major decisions were shared. I remember telling Marion that I was doing something I had never done before. Almost every noon hour I would walk from my office to the Eaton Center for lunch. Immediately, with her laser-like intuition, Marion replied: "Your soul is getting ready to leave St. Michael's." After many wonderful, creative years, the politics eventually became intolerable. Struggling with my decision to leave, Marion's advice was, "Well, Elinor, do what you always do—just keep blowing your feather in the wind and following it." Along with the image of the Tarot card and the symbolic image of the white feather blowing in the wind at the beginning and end of the movie, *Forrest Gump,* I could only say,

"Marion that is the archetypal symbol of the fool!" "Well, if the shoe fits, ---!" Teasing aside, she was referring to my own intuition, informed by instinct that gives rise to the inner voice with its own logic around decision making. At least, I think she was! In fact, the convergence of events in the next few months made my leaving St. Michael's Hospital easy on every level.

During this time, Marion had a deep desire to use the money from her books and lectures to establish a Jung Institute in Toronto. In the early '90s, she had been looking at property in the vicinity of St. Clair and Avenue Road with the intent to buy. I remember one long evening sitting around my dining room table with an architect looking at a set of plans and possible renovations that would accommodate a library, lecture hall, and offices. Having been convinced of the feasibility of such a plan, she put in an offer on a property with the condition it would need approval from the others involved. When she presented it to the other analysts, my understanding is there was not only no interest, but much resistance to the plan. Despite the depth of our friendship, there were times when Marion was sparse in her explanations. I speculated that part of this resistance was likely due to the practicality of undertaking both the responsibility and expense of running an institute: taxes, repairs, et cetera; but I detected another sticking point around Marion's insistence of bringing the body through the door and particularly the way in which she worked with it. My impression at the time, was this resistance extended even to Zurich. In any case, a permanent residence for the Jung Institute in Toronto was not to be. Marion phoned me the following evening to say everything was off. I could hear the disappointment in her voice. It often happens that we can have good intentions, but the way forward is blocked. We can only surrender to Sophia's choreography. Sometimes the universe has a different vision of where our energy needs to go.

One of the ways her energy wanted to go presented itself to Marion around 2002. With Mary Hamilton and Ann Skinner, the Body/Soul Intensives, started some years before, had grown with an increasing number of participants. The Leadership Training program had been established and many participants were calling for a more formal structure in the form of The Woodman Foundation. This request came at a time when Marion was thinking about cutting back on the many requests she received to give talks at major conferences around the world. While she would always teach, she wanted to focus her energy more on working in depth with women; going from talking about body/soul to trying to actualize a deeper feminine consciousness.

From our early discussions about the Foundation, I recall Marion's doubt on at least two levels. Rooted in the feminine process of creative transformation, initially, at least, she did not favor the granting of a certificate or setting up a degree program. It was the degree of surrender to the archetypal energies wanting to come through that needed to be sufficiently incarnated. Those who have been faithful to their own work will go on to become creative centers within themselves and the work of feminine consciousness will continue. If this energy is not incarnated and expressed through them, their work will fall by the wayside. I recall Marion saying: "they will either have it or they won't. No piece of paper can give them that."

When it came to the Foundation there was the optics. In truth, I think how the Foundation would be perceived within the larger Jungian community pressed on me more than any thought Marion had about it. At the time it seemed to me that Marion was more concerned about the temptation of those involved in the Foundation to revert to structure rather than process. While one may strive for self-organizing, or ecological structures, patriarchal structures are still deeply engraved in our psyche, making it easy to go there. What made the Foundation appealing to her was the argument that by using her name, money could be raised for scholarships allowing the intensives to be open to more people. The possibility of making the work more available to more people seemed to me one of the deciding factors in her decision to say "yes."

I can make no subjective statements about the Foundation or the Body/Soul Intensives as I was never personally involved in them. The above is only my recollection of the many conversations we had about this topic at the time, and the fact that I agreed with her that the format of the Intensives was a powerful therapeutic tool that would change and evolve in an organic fashion, or not, depending on the vision and soul connection of those within it.

Decisions often reflect our embodied values. One day in the early '90s, I remember sitting at the dining-room table at Walmer Road looking over a talk Marion was going to give. The phone rang, and Marion went into her bedroom to take the call. When she came out she looked at me with a quizzical smile. A major publisher in the United States had phoned to propose sending an editor to work with her for a few months, expense free, to help her write in the manner of some of the popular "gurus" of the time. With a reconfiguring of her message, she could have best sellers. Many of us are not faced with the temptation to fame and fortune, and Marion could have seen it as "getting her work out there." But for Marion it was an easy choice. I never said it, but I truly loved, admired, her in that moment. Her integrity and clarity about the process of feminine consciousness and how it is expressed could not be comprised.

If we are open to the unconscious depths, the most direct route to decision making can come in our dreams. Marion has spoken of the persistent dreams propelling her to resign from her beloved teaching and go to Zurich. For both Marion and me our dreams were often very precise. We lived from them, made many decisions based on them realizing, ultimately, that in some mysterious way our destiny was being laid out for us. Most of the decisions we made were against the background of being guided from deep within our own body/soul.

When it came to making decisions, Marion loved my image of Maat in which the heart is weighed in the balance against a feather from the goddess' headdress. One day she went to the museum and tracked down a copy of this image of Maat for me. On the back she wrote: "I often think of you in my own decision making with this image in mind." She told me that she saw me as a woman who has lived her life knowing that her heart is being weighed against the feather of truth, taking responsibility for that, and living my truth accordingly. While I hope my decisions are made against the feather of truth, I know Marion's decisions, always deeply intuitive, ultimately flowed from the heart.

PART III

SPIRALING OUT:
LOVE IN ACTION

SEVEN

The Black Madonna...is black because she's unknown to consciousness. She is nature impregnated, accepting her own body as the chalice of Spirit.

Marion

The spiritual quest for wholeness was the underlying passion of both our lives, a passion that grew in clarity as the years passed. We had become part of an ongoing, *conscious* process of incarnation, and for this to happen we had to learn to handle the energy that wants to come in creatively. On an individual level, if this creative engagement doesn't happen there is a risk that we will fall back into old projections, complexes, or other neurotic symptoms. The same is true when the container exists between two (or more) people. The shared energy must be at the disposal of the creative process. That is, openness to the archetypal images coming in and their creative expression becomes imperative if a healthy, transformative relationship is to continue to evolve. Enfolded within the deep love and trust that formed the container between us, it was this creative tension that sustained the interwoven expression of our friendship and our ongoing work.

Following my analysis, for the next ten years our interest became centered on an emerging image that eventually led to publishing *Dancing in the Flames*. For those who know Marion's work, I was

DANCING AT THE STILL POINT

obviously playing catch-up when it came to the Black Madonna. Marion began to dream of the Black Madonna, but she was to encounter her in incarnate form in India. Many times, Marion has told the story of sitting in the lobby of the Ashoka Hotel ill and in culture shock. She sat down at one end of a couch trying to write a letter. A large, dark-skinned Indian woman came and sat down next to her pressing her arm and shoulder into Marion. When Marion moved down the couch the woman would move with her and soon they were at the other end of the couch, pressed against each other. Each day she would go to the lobby the same dignified lady appeared and the ritual would repeat itself. Then one morning, a man approached them and said, "you are all right now." Marion was startled, but he went on to explain that he had recognized the aloneness that comes with dying and had asked his wife to sit with her until her body came back into life. Marion muttered her stunned "thank you" as the couple walked away.

Spiraling into deeper and more meaningful insights, by the time Marion wrote *Addiction to Perfection* she was beginning to grasp the archetypal image of the Black Madonna as the necessary counterpoint to the idealized, disembodied Madonna image worshipped by the patriarchal church. Marion writes of her challenge having to reconcile her Christian inheritance with bringing the Black Madonna into consciousness, just as in my analysis, my Christian understanding of the Virgin brought the black "Shambat" into consciousness.

Historically, we need to remember this split in feminine energy was not always the case. Mary was said to have gone to Ephesus after the death of Her Son and the Church dedicated to Her was built over the great temple of Artemis. In the early Church, people associated Mary with the virgin goddess who hunted by moonlight but was also the protector of children and women in childbirth. When the Church tried to demote Mary, the people of Ephesus rioted in the street demanding that Mary be given the title Mother of God. They not only demanded a Goddess but one that, over the centuries, was increasingly embodied. Across Europe the worship of the Black Madonna was widespread up until the late Middle Ages. It was only after the Great Mortality, the great plague of the 14th century and our attempts to control irrational nature, including women, that the Virgin became whitewashed and worshipped from afar. Although Catholics still call Mary the Mother of God, the symbolism has been reduced to formula and the meaning largely lost. Now it seems this great archetypal energy is coming back into the culture through our dreams.

When she came to write *The Pregnant Virgin,* Marion devoted a whole section to "The Black Madonna." She became aware that as women began to deal with the unconscious aspects of their psyche, the shadow and the complexes, particularly the mother complex, they could begin to open up to more transpersonal forces. As the body awakens, the experience of the positive mother, of Sophia, begins to emerge. Marion recognized that the release of the trauma buried in the body often resulted in dreams of a black goddess that could bridge body and soul. The Black Madonna is the intersection of sexuality and spirituality, the emerging soul through whom the creative flow of new life is struggling to be born.

Working through the resonance in my own body, Sophia was gently guiding me into a deeper knowledge of the feminine principle. One of my first introductions to the Dark Goddess resulted from my first visit to Sha Sha. The island, said to be a gift to an Indigenous princess, left me with a dream the morning of my return. In my dream, there is an ancient tree standing in the middle of the island. Its branches are laden with green leaves that were all curled up. My task was to gently unfurl each leaf and free the gold butterflies inside. I was being instructed to release the soul within nature, the light within matter.

For about a month I kept looking for references to "the butterfly tree." The tree appears in every kind of symbolism but no butterfly tree. About a month later in a chance visit to the neighborhood bookstore I finally found a book about the butterfly tree, *Jaguar Woman and the Wisdom of the Butterfly Tree,* written by Lynn Andrews. I should not have been surprised that it was an Indigenous story of the Tree Mother and helped expand my understanding of the archetypal feminine and her role in our transformation. This is not the tree in Eden, or what we have come to think of as the *axis mundi*. The branches of this tree contain billions of leaves and on each one is written the destiny of a person. When we are born a leaf falls from the tree and our spirit journey, our destiny, is to consciously realize that we are all one with the sacred tree. On the ancient island of Sha Sha, I was reminded through Indigenous teaching that not only are we one with all creation, but our destiny is to realize that we are the light of the Butterfly Tree, the light of Sophia in Nature. Also, the dream made clear that, as a therapist, it is my task to help release that light in nature and in the body.

Often what crosses our path is also part of the ongoing choreography of Sophia. In 1986 I was asked to give workshops to groups of about 25–30 women. The myth that presented itself to me as the backdrop for this workshop was that of Aphrodite and Psyche. It was a workshop I would repeat several times and remains among the most potent workshops I have ever done. Many women can identify with the death marriage and/or the unconscious marriage. Others identified with Psyche's need to honor her own agenda and, when necessary, not get involved in saving everyone else. At another level, many resonated with Aphrodite's words when Psyche finally seeks her out. Chiding Psyche, she says, "Well, you finally remembered you have a Goddess." Many women were (are) remembering they have a Goddess. She not only teaches us the source of our true beauty, but She teaches us "under pain of death" the need to develop our masculine energy; to prepare for the inner marriage in order that the divine marriage can take place in the transpersonal realm.

It is the feminine container of life that must be transformed. As all traditions attest, this transformation takes a period of intense and focused awareness. Although feminine and masculine energies constantly reveal each other, a conscious feminine must precede the birth of a new conscious masculine. At different times Marion and I would discuss these themes. As a clinical psychologist, I knew that the defenses we use: denial, repression, intellectualization, et cetera, conform to the time of our wounding. Coming from the viewpoint of eating disorders and other addictions, Marion had become aware that if the trauma is very early—before consciousness can even register it—such constricting energy must be worked with in the body. This is particularly true if the body/soul split began *in utero* where the fetus was unwanted or the "wrong" gender.

Focused on the mother/daughter myth of Demeter/Persephone, Marion's early Intensives were powerful, and the experience of the women attending them was profound—as my clients would inform me. The evidence became apparent in the qualitative shift in their dreams. The Mother Complex rooted in the Great Mother is so deep in our psyche and so disfigured by years of patriarchal repression, it requires many women to dive deep and face their fears of abandonment or messages of "not being good enough." It is only when this work of establishing the receptive feminine container for life is undertaken that the need for a new masculine energy can make itself felt.

The time came when Marion knew the tenure of the Intensives must shift to a new myth, the Aphrodite/Psyche myth. Aphrodite's demanding tutelage is aimed at strengthening our inner masculine, developing our ability to analyze and discriminate, to be assertive, to engage a larger vision of life and be able to relate the part to the whole. Finally, we need a mature masculine to be able to focus on our journey into the depths and bring Beauty back into the world. Marion was aware that while women had worked fiercely on achieving a greater feminine consciousness, when certain issues or disagreements came up, they would frequently fall back into the old patriarchal ways of doing things or they became over-sensitized to what they perceived as the power of others. We observed that women with an immature masculine typically feel oppressed or become manipulative when anyone has power over them. It takes a mature masculine to uphold the feminine values rooted in love and calmly stand to one's own truth. I became more aware of why, in 1986, I had intuitively chosen this myth as the basis for my own workshops. Quite simply, my wounding had taken place in adolescence, a time of shaming when I needed support for going out into the world and learning to stand in my own truth.

By the 1990s, I got the impression Marion was simply tired of having to be "Mother." Teasingly she would say to me, "How come you get to appear in dreams as White Buffalo Woman, or a Medieval Sorcerer, or the Keeper of the Sacred Canoe, or Artemis. I'm not really Mother, you know!" I totally agreed. "You come out with truths right from the shoulder, but you also have warmth and an inviting energy that is attractive to many people." Marion had just returned from a workshop with Robert Bly. Robert was away on the Saturday and Marion was left working with the men she had worked with on many occasions. "Elinor, I could sense the mother projection floating around the room, and my frustration reached its limit. I had to be very direct in saying that I didn't want to carry that projection." The men became agitated, saying things like, "That is what we need. You can't change that!" "Well, I can," she said. "I'm not there anymore."

While Marion was present to where people were, in these remarks, I heard Marion's desire to work with men, and women, at a deeper level of spiritual maturity. In *Dancing in the Flames,* we wrote two chapters: "Telling it Like It Is," followed by "And a Crone Shall Lead Them." The Crone stands between death and new life. She is about transformation. In "Telling it Like It Is" I presented the journeys of two men I worked with over four or five years. To make a generalization, most men will back away from engaging in deep process, particularly when the images presented are very dark or challenging. If they can suffer the Crone energy, as Parsifal had to suffer the challenge of the hag Kundry, they can go deep and far in finding the Grail. Of course, as the therapist, I often got that projection. For my part, I saw it as tough love.

Projections carry real energy. Hopefully, one can negotiate these projections creatively during analysis and come to a point where they start to fall by the wayside. On occasion when one is carrying the projection of the Self, particularly as the Good Mother, the energy can easily swing into the snake-headed Medusa. That is, if the mother wound is touched, however inadvertently, the explosion can be frightening. The result can be shattering for both client and therapist. Having had that experience, Marion could guide me through it. In a way I had not grasped before, I learned the potential danger of carrying archetypal projections and the care that one must take for both analyst and client.

The workshops I led on Aphrodite and Psyche revealed different aspects of the unconscious feminine psyche, from the true meaning of beauty to the acceptance of a natural sexuality. I found that while many women have a longing for and deep anger toward Mother, often they do not fear her as deeply as they fear their repressed Aphrodite, the Goddess of Love and Beauty. Throughout history many women have unconsciously identified with Her and used their beauty to survive by means of seduction and manipulation, which is a power that dissipates with age. Other women unconsciously measure themselves against an ideal of outer beauty that leads them to envy an unattainable body image. Men, throughout literature and in real life, desire and curse her. Without a differentiated consciousness, Aphrodite can lead women, and men, into destructive relationships. While it may be under threat of death, it is out of love that Aphrodite lays out a path to bring our creative masculine energy into consciousness. This is the union between masculine and feminine that must take place before Beauty and Joy can be birthed into the world.

It became clear to me that before real masculine transformation can take place in a woman, the Dark Goddess, embodying instinctual and spiritual energy, must be present. In the psychic fields we create between us, as I was developing my own understanding of feminine consciousness both within and without, my clients, women and men, were able to open to their own deeper understanding of the feminine and particularly her tutoring and healing role. Among many of the Black Goddess dreams that we wrote about in *Dancing in The Flames*, for me it was the revelation of two dreams that demanded writing about the emergence of this energy happening in our culture. A client of mine, Anne, was so disembodied that her University colleagues were afraid her thoughts were becoming confabulated. One of her first dreams showed a large trunk in the basement which she proceeded to unpack layer by layer. At the very bottom she found little creatures that she identified as teardrops. After some time of working with me and doing bodywork with Beverly Stokes, Anne had a dream whose images seem to speak to the whole psyche/soma process as envisioned by Marion.

In the dream, Anne is walking alone on the moor at dusk when she is opened up to the numinous. A larger-than-life black woman with flowing black robes and hair is walking toward her. Anne is very nervous and tries to go back but there is no escaping Her. Surrender is the only way out. The Goddess figure takes her by the hand and they make their way toward a beautiful, round, sparkling house set among evergreen trees. Inside, there is an extraordinary mandala on the floor with vivid colors of tangerine, gold, and azure blue. Anne moves to the center of the mandala as a strong container will be necessary for the outpouring of the unconscious transforming energies she is about to experience. Suddenly a seven-foot-tall ebony carving shoots up from the middle of the mandala and grasps her hand. Immediately, the carving transforms into a flow of brilliantly colored gossamer-like material kept in shape solely by the resonating sound of the music. Finally, the column turns into a fountain of water and Anne finds herself naked, totally herself, and dancing in the clear, refreshing spray.

In allowing her energy to flow from the depths of the un-conscious, Anne opens her body to new vibrational possibilities, safe within the resonating womb. She is vulnerable but unencumbered.

Her initiation by the Goddess into the feminine mystery leads Anne to the navel of existence. The dark wood becomes the crystal fountain. The energy rising from the roots of existence is transformed from the dark matter of the Great Mother to the translucent matter of the Goddess. At a deeper, archetypal level this dream points to the Fountain of Life flowing in four directions from the center of Paradise. To open to this inner fountain is to be transformed by its life-giving water.

A second dream that coalesced in my mind at this time was a dream that Marion often spoke about with great delight. The dreamer is standing by the seashore, the edge between consciousness and the unconscious depths. On the horizon, she sees a great tidal wave approaching. She panics. Gradually, she discerns a large, black woman riding triumphantly on the crest of the wave her arm upheld in triumph. As the dreamer's panic turns to surrender, she realizes she is a molecule of energy in the wave and surrounded by her friends. They are all molecules in the wave, and each molecule is dancing with every other molecule in love. They are all dancing with the momentum of the wave that will bring Sophia to land.

While Anne's dream reveals the deep inner body/soul transformation necessary at a personal level allowing us to dance at the still point, Marion's dream speaks to the Goddess's role in bringing the immense, feminine energy, so long repressed, into our culture. We both realized that individually and collectively, She is pushing through our unconscious, the living feminine energy capable of transforming life as we know it.

In 2015, I saw Her image galvanized in the thousands of dark-skinned women protesting in the streets of India. They were affirming their humanity and their rights in the face of the widespread rape and violence that would rob them of their voice, their dignity, and even their life. The creative power of the black woman is coming to the fore in many places.

Aware of Marion's deep insights into this energy and the dreams I was now gathering, it seemed a book would be an appropriate vessel to share the messages we were being given, both personally and through the field of our clients. While reading the Toronto newspaper one morning, an article on the opening of a temple dedicated to the dark, fierce, Hindu goddess, Kali, I thought a good title would be *Dancing in the Flames*. Slowly, a book was beginning to take shape, but there would be many hurdles before it came to fruition. A book about the Black Goddess would be unthinkable without Marion's deep insight into this emerging image that had shaped her life over the past fifteen years, but in 1993–1994, Sophia presented Marion with a different challenge.

EIGHT

Repressed energy returns to haunt us in symbol and symptom.

Marion

One evening in 1999, Marion made her way over to my place to deliver into my hands the first finished draft of *Bone: Dying into Life.* I remember that evening very well. It represented the closure of a harrowing journey I was privileged to be part of. Receiving this manuscript from Marion felt like a communion silently celebrated together.

In November 1993, Marion received a diagnosis of endometrial cancer. When one feels healthy there is shock and disbelief at such a diagnosis. At first it seemed hopeful. It would mean major surgery, but if it had not spread, life could resume as usual. Her doctors operated but afterward they were not sure if the cancer had penetrated the uterine wall. The doctors decided that massive radiation would be needed. I had difficulty reading *Bone* because it brought back the same visceral response I had in the face of the incompetent medical practices that Marion was subjected to in London. If only . . . her situation, even today, would be quite different in many respects. Having access to many specialists in Toronto, I learned it is standard practice to remove several lymph nodes as part of a hysterectomy when cancer is involved. If this is not done you have no idea if the cancer has spread through the wall and it is a procedure that can't be done after the fact. Apparently, they did not biopsy the lymph nodes and so had no idea if it had penetrated beyond the uterine wall or not.

Marion and I talked on the phone every week during the weeks of radiation. The procedures I was hearing about seemed draconian to me. While outwardly trying to keep a calm demeanor, inwardly there were days I could feel my insides turning to ice. Talking with a prominent radiologist in Toronto, I was told that if a set of X-rays was given to the radiology department of most large hospitals across Canada, it is likely that London would be the odd one out in their interpretation.

Along with the seeming incompetence of the medical care, another difficulty I had reading *Bone* was a subtext that had filled me with dread and that I was now seeing played out. Prior to Marion's medical procedures I had a long and wrenching dream. In the dream, Marion is going back to the land of Nod, her hometown, and at the end of the dream she is lying on a steel slab while a demon lover figure is splaying her open. Not knowing the outcome of the medical procedures at the time, I was almost embarrassed by the clarity and ferocity of the dream. It took a few days and a lot of reflection before I mentioned it to Marion and asked her to reconsider and receive her medical treatment in Toronto. While she seemed to take my dream seriously, the decision had been made. I didn't press her but the whole incident remains conflicted within me to this day.

With excruciating pain in her back and difficulty walking, Marion returned to the hospital in London only to receive a second diagnosis. As Marion writes in *Bone*, "Dr. MacNeil, a quiet, unprepossessing man, comes in. He says he read the scan with the other doctors. They agree it is metastasized bone cancer on the inside of my sacrum."[9] This was confirmed by a second doctor who felt there was no need for a biopsy. It was certainly cancer. His prognosis was two months to two years with less time rather than more. The only thing to do was more radiation—for palliative purposes.

I felt Marion should see someone at Princess Margaret Hospital and began to make some phone calls. At the same time, Marion had a dear friend in California, Jill Mellick, who, as she wrote about, was more successful in arranging for a second opinion with a radiologist at Stanford Medical Center, Dr. Bob Mindelzun. This intervention

---

[9] Woodman, Marion. *Bone,* op. cit., p.178.

changed the energy and the trajectory Marion was on. Dr. Mindelzun affirmed that there was osteoporosis and osteoarthritis along with a collection of fluid but there did not seem to be any malignant process. He continued to explain everything to her and explained how she needed a gynecologist and an oncologist. Marion finally did see Dr. Fyles at Princess Margaret Hospital who ordered a new MRI. Apparently even the MRI done in London wasn't satisfactory! A new MRI was done at Princess Margaret and the diagnosis of Dr. Mindelzun at Stanford was confirmed by Dr. Flyes: severe osteoarthritis, but no cancer.

Visiting Marion in hospital after that first operation in November 1993, I agreed with her that she did not need to be "out there" as much as she had previously. She no longer needed to be "mother." She also confided in me that Ross had been in earlier that day to have her sign the papers to purchase the property on Sydenham; a property he had his eye on for some time had just become available. Marion had not seen the property, and, at that time, she still had some reluctance in moving to London full time. As we talked, she became reconciled with the idea by entertaining the option of renting a studio apartment in London where she could go and work during the day. It seems, while Ross was brilliant and energetic, his boundaries could be challenging. As it turned out, her plan to rent a separate studio was abandoned as it seemed Sydenham had a sufficiently long hallway between her office and Ross's—and she still had her Toronto apartment. The extreme pain in her back and difficulty in walking had persuaded Marion to give up her office on St. Clair but her need to maintain a connection in Toronto meant that Walmer Road would remain for several more years.

The reason her medical ordeal comes up at this time in my writing about our relationship is that, during our weekly phone calls, I could feel Marion psychically slipping away. In her own words: "My rational mind has accepted that I do not have cancer, my unconsciousness is still trapped in a death wish... In almost every issue I can let go, but I am terrified of chaos."[10] Trauma often reasserts the old patterns of the ego, even when we are aware of what is happening. Since we cannot just decree the ego to let go, we need to move deeper into the body—learn to walk again, or rather to dance.

---

[10] Ibid., p. 216

When the body is in pain, it is sometimes necessary to keep the mind focused on something, to find the creative order in the chaos, an order that enlarges the vision. It was for this reason I suggested we collaborate on a book, *Dancing in the Flames*. (The title deeply resonated with her, and she later asked if she could use it for a movie Adam Reid was making of her life.) I had been writing away, doing "case studies" with some of my clients, and writing not only of the role of the Dark Goddess in the process of transformation but also of the transformation of the Goddess herself as she is successively revealed through our emerging consciousness. Slowly, Marion responded with her own writing, even taking on the challenge of chaos. In the midst of this process, I remember sitting in her living room at Walmer Road, she in a chair and I across the room on the sofa. There was a huge, ominous energy between us as our unspoken words were tuned to the fact that this book might be published posthumously. A few months later we learned that death was not in the cards, at least not for now.

I thought I was being rather sneaky, gently tempting her to focus her energy by writing, but at the book launching I had to laugh as she acknowledged with gratitude exactly what I had done. Along with the book, the underlying triumph of that time is, perhaps, best expressed in the picture below.

Marion and Elinor at the book launching arranged by Knopf Canada.

The day of the book launching remains in my memory, as it captured so many aspects of our friendship; the humor, the love, and the sharing with friends both in real life and, as it turned out, in dreams. Early that morning, we engaged in an hour-long radio interview on a very popular CBC program. As we left the studio and were walking toward my car, I mentioned to Marion that I was thinking of speaking that evening on the more light-hearted aspects of writing together, and, more seriously, on her return. This was her first public appearance since the cancer. With her best mischievous smile, she looked at me and replied, "You can say anything you like; just remember I'm speaking after you."

Later, we met at my place for lunch. Before sitting down to eat, Marion pulled out a beautifully wrapped box. Earlier, she had gone to her safety-deposit box and removed some valued treasures that she had left me in her will but wanted to give them to me on this occasion. I was dumbstruck! Lunch was followed by a ritual in which we let the book go out into the world. It no longer belonged to us. Following this, Marion became very introverted, even shy, and in a low voice told me how much our friendship meant to her. My even more introverted feeling, often awkward in articulating the inner depths, managed to both receive and affirm the deep love and creativity that flowed between us.

On reflection, it was that day that I learned from Marion the true meaning of ritual. It was not only sending the book out into the world, but part of the ritual was also the gift with which she honored our friendship. When an intention is rooted in Love, its expression is the essence of ritual.

While the book launching that evening was a wonderful celebration with over a hundred invited guests, the celebration didn't stop there. What remains a vivid memory for me are the dreams that I learned about in the following days. There were two distinct themes. Over the following week, three or four women sent me dreams centered round the "golden threads" that were being woven in order to join everyone in the room. In one instance the dreamer was in the room and as Marion and I were talking, she noticed that everyone was transparent. She could see a gold ball where the heart would be and from it were strings of gold connecting everyone in the room. Images of the web of life, of the golden threads, are in all cultures and speak to the interconnectedness of all things. This response to the book still fills me with a sense of reverence; an occasion to bow one's head.

The men also had a theme, including Ross and Marion's lawyer. They dreamt of a great medieval banquet hall where much feasting was going on. I can only speculate that since the Black Madonna was so prominent in medieval times, a time before we lost our soul in the split between spirit and matter, they were escorted back there to begin the healing.

The reviewers were mostly positive but the real measure of the book for us was what it had stirred up in the unconscious. We had many letters from women but also from men. One sent us an essay affirming the emergence of Dionysus; a Chicago businessman was having repeated dreams of a large black woman and wondered if we could recommend an analyst in the vicinity, while another, a physicist from New Zealand was enthusiastic of the overall thesis of the book. You never know where the spirit will blow.

In the summer of 2014 when I entered Marion's room, she was sitting reading a copy of *Dancing in the Flames.* Stroking the inside page, she looked up at me and said, "This is very beautiful, Elinor." She was referring to what I had written in the front of the book many years ago as we had dedicated a copy to each other.

Sitting there in her room I said, "This book was born out of a lot of love." She could remember my using it to help pull her into life, and I recalled her concern about publishing it. That is, at least three times she said to me, "Are you sure you want to do this? You know they will put my name first and all the fuss will be directed at me. I want you to be very sure you are okay with that. I don't want any shadow stuff seeping into our relationship." Like many other occasions I was privy to, Marion's integrity never ceased to amaze me. On that day, she just smiled and said, "That is how Sophia works."

NINE

Sometimes [the Black Madonna] has a son with her. He, too, is an outcast—outcast by the power principle that can only destroy our global village. Her son is an image of potential masculinity, which is very different from what we generally associate with patriarchy...If we ever bring the Black Madonna's son to consciousness our idea of mature masculinity will be revolutionized.

Marion

In reflecting on masculine consciousness, I am inclined to call this section "The Book We Never Wrote." A few years after the publication of *Dancing in the Flames*, I recall a discussion Marion and I had one evening about masculine consciousness; where it was at the time, and what the unconscious, particularly through dreams, was trying to bring into the culture. Earlier, in 1990, Marion published a book on the masculine in women, *The Ravaged Bridegroom*. Twenty-seven years ago, it did not elicit the same enthusiastic response as her earlier writing on the feminine. Over the years, she became dissatisfied with the book and remarked on different occasions that she would like to rewrite it. Personally, I found the material full of deep insight and could point out many passages and conclusions that I found enlightening. Today, I would encourage anyone to read her thesis outlined in the first chapter. As usual, Marion had deep insight into the personal and collective work that needs to be done.

One of our discussions about the masculine centered around a talk she had given at St. Paul's Church in 1989, "Lover, Can You Spare a Dime?" That talk symbolized for Marion her own personal break from patriarchy, from her father as minister of a patriarchal God. It was not lost on her that she had come full circle, because there she was standing at the pulpit of this large church in downtown Toronto delivering a talk that denounced patriarchy. Through her deep inner work, Marion had rejected patriarchy and had made great strides in bringing a new feminine into consciousness, both personally and culturally. But since we have lived in a patriarchal paradigm going back some 5,000 years, its scripts are not easy to set aside and even harder to transform. For years, Marion worked with women deeply dedicated to finding their true voice, their own feminine consciousness, but she would have to remind them that often when the occasion came to move out into the world, to make certain decisions, they could easily slip right back into unconscious patriarchy.

That night in 1989, Marion talked of experiencing a terror and a deeper rage than ever before, recalling how she and many of the people she was working with, men and women had struggled to free themselves from the stranglehold patriarchal power principles had on them. She talked about the crumbling of patriarchy; about the values that were taken for granted for centuries and are now being questioned as we watch our raped planet wither under the pressures of acid rain, toxic waste, exploitation. Early on, Marion understood the relationship between the environment and the outdated structures of patriarchy, especially the ideology behind capitalism.

From her talk, she recalled the dream of a male analysand she called Tom, that symbolized the Great Mother being turned into the Black Goddess while Viking warriors, Tom's instinctual energy, does away with the old patriarchal image of Christ. These dreams reminded me of my own encounter with Dionysus and the need for a new masculine energy to come into the culture.

Arriving at Walmer Road that evening, Marion jumped out of the car, and our lives flowed out into the light of another day and the separate work we were both involved in. For Marion, Body/Soul Intensives engaged more and more of her time and energy. The year 1992 saw the publication of *Leaving My Father's House,* to be followed by *Conscious Femininity* in 1993. For an upcoming award, I once made a list for Marion of the audio and video tapes she made during this time. The count at that time was something like 83–85 audio tapes and four videotapes including *Healing Spirit* (with Bernie Siegel and Deepak Chopra); *Who is Hungry for What?* A New Medicine Tape; *Every Inch a Queen, Cancer as a Turning Point: Surviving to Thriving*; and *Men and Women* (with Robert Bly); a six-part television documentary series. Of course, there were articles in books with titles such as *Betwixt and Between: Rites of Initiation; Pre and Perinatal Psychology; Family Secrets: Life Stories of Adult Children of Alcoholics; To Be a Woman: Conscious Femininity: Mother, Virgin, Crone; We Two: Embracing the Dark; On Women Turning 60: Embracing the Age of Fulfillment.* A bibliography of articles in journals and magazines becomes extensive. Journals range from Common Boundary, The Bloomsbury Review, Noetic Sciences Review, Infocus, M.E.N. magazine, and at least three different articles i n the United Kingdom's medical journal Caduceus. Many others have been published in art magazines. She lectured at the Ontario College of Art on two occasions and twice at International Art Therapy Conferences. When the Edvard Munch Exhibit was brought to the Art Gallery of Ontario, Marion was asked to do the taped commentary on his work for visitors touring the exhibit. As all great art comes out of core imagery and essence, a realm she knows so well, she was delighted to fulfill this request. To say Marion was prolific in her creativity would be an understatement.

My own creativity was more focused during the period 1989–1993, as I continued as Chief of Psychological Services at St. Michael's hospital as well as sustaining a large private analytic practice. I did give many lectures, including two memorial lectures at the University of

Toronto. I also conducted weekend workshops on various Jungian-related topics in Montreal, Toronto, and other areas around Ontario. The wildest and most fun-filled workshop I ever did was a weekend at the University in Newfoundland while some of the most challenging were in the northern States. Following a seminar on the emerging paradigm beyond patriarchy that I gave in Toronto at the Center for Compassionate Leadership, some of the participants requested the themes be developed in a series of smaller workshops. Out of these discussions came a series of 22 weekend workshops that took place over the next ten years. Marcella and Eldon Shields, psychologists from the United States, had been invited to Canada to set up the Compassionate Leadership Program. Both had done Jungian analysis and had a deep spiritual orientation. We all had large analytic practices, and we agreed that a great deal needed to be done outside the limitations of the office setting. We needed to work with the body and with the imagination in different ways. Marcella had a gift for incorporating archetypal energies into experiential exercises and some of the participants could be called upon for bodywork, mask making, et cetera. We also agreed that the workshops would be loosely based on what was coming into consciousness within the field of our clients and that we would work with both men and women. "Women and Men: The Journey Together" became a community built on shared vulnerability and compassion. From the wounded child, to the Fool, to a weekend spent relating from our shadow side, these workshops generated a great deal of energy, very supportive of the whole analytic process.

During the years that followed the publication of *Dancing in the Flames* I became aware of another image appearing in the dreams of my clients. I began to collect dreams that spoke powerfully of a black man, or a dark stranger. These dreams resonated with my own journey; the transformation of the black-cloaked devil into the dark-haired Dionysus. I remembered Jung's encounter with the dark-skinned man that helped him slay the old heroic thinking pattern of his culture. I thought of physicist Wolfgang Pauli's dreams of the dark stranger that wanted to be admitted into the halls of academia, who wanted to teach him the music that gave fluidity and form to the notes. I even recalled one of my favorite Westerns starring Clint Eastwood in "Pale Rider"—the solitary stranger who rides into the valley: the preacher sitting tall on his horse holding a stick of dynamite. He stirs things up but eventually heals the split between masculine and feminine, between husband and wife, and between brute force and compassion in the community.

As the Dark Goddess becomes embodied as the transitional energy in the psyche, the Dark God will make his appearance. Certainly, this energy was manifesting in the dreams of my patients. To complement *Dancing in the Flames*, I started to compile the dreams I was collecting, along with my thoughts, under the title *Desirer-of-Life* taken from an ancient Nordic manuscript, the *Voluspar* or Priestess' Prophecy. After the upheaval caused by war, power struggles, and fanaticism, this prophecy tells us that there will be a new dispensation. Woman will be known as Life and man as the Desirer-of-Life. The relationship between men and women will take on a new, creative meaning extending to all the land. The dark stranger dreams of my clients seemed to circle around order and chaos, the light in nature, and the bringing of fluidity and movement into a world mired in matter.

One client, Helen, dreamt she was at the university sitting next to a man seated at a computer. He was showing her the intricacy of its logic. She was very bored. This was a man she knew in real life to be very precise, obsessive, nit-picking, almost an exaggeration of the disembodied masculine, the "head" man. In the dream she looks up and there is a tall, black man entering the room. He is just standing there in the doorway. She leaves the man with the computer and moves toward the door. Although she is drawn toward the stranger, she is very apprehensive and moves cautiously past him. In her need to get everything right, Helen acted in the world with an obsessive attention to detail that left her exhausted. This dark stranger heralded the presence of a new energy that could balance her order with passion.

Even the presence of this energy in dreams stirs up attraction and fear even if he first appears quite passive. His hidden energy quivers with uncertainty. At other times he may appear full force in the form of a gypsy lover, or a highwayman who abducts her from her coach and rides off with her to a night of music, dancing, and wild love-making. In one woman's dream he appears as a dark-hooded man wanting to be released but the woman is too unconscious, too immature to risk releasing him.

Another amazing set of dreams had to do with the spirit in matter, the dark stranger rising up out of the earth bringing fluidity and motion into our psyche and into a culture that has been rendered concrete and leaden. One woman writes in her dream journal:

> I am standing in an ancient forest grove when, suddenly, my eyes focus on a huge moss-covered stone. As the ground begins to shake under my feet, the stone slowly moves. Out of the earth rises a large black man. He appears numinous and I am transfixed by his presence.

In dreams of other women, the dark stranger comes out of a deep well or from within a cave. The dreamer is transformed by the light in his eyes or he takes her into an embrace and she feels all her energy being released.

In still another dream there is an earthquake and as the ground splits open a dark man emerges from the earth.

Like the dark stranger in Pauli's dreams, he wants to teach us the music, the interconnected flow of life, not just the notes. In one woman's dream a great church celebration is taking place:

> _Everything_ is happening. But from out of the cast-of-thousands singing and dancing, a special "event" emerges. A strong black man, with great big white teeth, began to sing all the bravura bass arias from Messiah: or if they weren't bass arias to start with, he sang them bass: "Let us break their bonds asunder," "for he is like a refiner's fire." _He was glorious!_

Similarly, another woman dreams that she is attending an outdoor lecture. A man is writing on a blackboard and it is very boring. Suddenly a larger-than-life black man walks up and takes the chalk. He begins writing, but the words fly off the blackboard and fill the air with music. Having worked hard to bring their feminine energy into consciousness, these women were now being asked to open to the dark stranger pressing to be brought into our culture.

This dark stranger also began to appear in the dreams of men. A man dreamt:

> *I am standing high above the town surrounded by an idyllic landscape. I am very high up and although I am on a wide, firm path, I have come to a dead end. I am standing at the edge of a steep cliff. A dark man comes toward me and I find this disquieting, but he leads me down another way back to the town.*

With a successful business and having come to an ideal, ordered place in his life, this man, now approaching mid-life suddenly finds he is at the edge of a cliff with nowhere else to go. In having attained the life he thought he wanted, he realizes he is cut off from life, cut off from the town, from others. But he cannot simply go back to the collective that he left. It will take the dark stranger to show him another way to insert himself back into life.

The images and dynamics of this dark, potentially *creative* masculine energy were some of the richest I have ever worked with. Destruction or liberation; this is an emerging masculine energy we need to engage and assimilate. For Marion, if he remains an outcast, he will seek to destroy the global village, and today his raging, violent destruction is scarily evident every time you turn on the television or pick up a paper. In our discussions, Marion was very open to rethinking *The Ravaged Bridegroom*. I wondered if between the earlier chapters on "Masculinity in Addictions," and "Cripples, Rebels, and Criminals" and the last two chapters on "The Bride and Bridegroom," there was something missing. As Marion rightly said, conscious femininity was just coming into consciousness; conscious masculinity was barely on the horizon. Perhaps, Marion's dissatisfaction with *The Ravaged Bridegroom* was that it was written too soon. That is, the positive life force of the dark masculine was only now appearing in dreams and in the collective field.

While the dark-skinned man or woman in dreams is an energetic image within our collective psyche, I always have thought it very telling that amidst the violence and killing fields of the 20th century it was the dark-skinned man who brought about one of the deepest changes in the masculine psyche for the good of the whole. Major political and social change came, not only through strength of conviction but through the power of non-violence, forgiveness, and reconciliation making their appearance in the form of Mahatma Gandhi, Martin Luther King, Jr., and Nelson Mandela.

Obviously, a book on evolving masculine consciousness was never undertaken. At the time, it slipped between the cracks as so many other things were coming into the field. I once thought of taking all Marion's recorded thoughts about the new masculine along with *Ravaged Bridegroom* and the dreams and thoughts I had collected and doing something with it. The purpose and outcome have not become clear to me either intuitively or in dreams and so, to date, I have not undertaken such a task. Intuitive people are notorious for moving on, so maybe that is the reason, or maybe it was just meant to be written by the two of us or by someone else. I really don't know. But as I began to write the next chapter I had to laugh as a further scenario presented itself.

TEN

Controversy becomes the testing ground of our integrity.
Elinor

As mentioned earlier, in 1994–1995 I gently pressed Marion to write *Dancing in the Flames* as a way of bringing her back into life following her cancer, a small step in continuing to fulfill her destiny. Although she dismissed it at the time, another ugly incident surfaced in 1995 through an article that appeared in "Saturday Night," an upscale monthly newsmagazine. Marion had willingly let herself be interviewed for this article, but I suspect, under false pretenses. It was published with the title "Running with the Wolf." Taking this article out of my files now, it strikes me as amusing in its bias. Knowing Marion's shadow, as she knew mine, I can be fairly "objective" if people are mystified or critical of her work. Reading this article just made me angry. Marion only shook her head and told me and others to forget about it as it wasn't worth the energy. I probably would have said the same if it had been about me but since it was about my friend, I wrote an icy letter to the editor clinically taking the article apart. Since my practice included several people in the literary and arts community, I knew that many others were equally incensed by the confused and venomous tone of the five-page article. The article began with a derogatory, mocking tone and left out quotes from Marion's friends, including me. It seems examples of Marion's authenticity and integrity did not fit with the narrative, while the words of others were twisted. One friend phoned Marion in tears explaining what she had really said and how it was misquoted. Instead, there were the unnamed sources afraid to comment because of Marion's power. To my knowledge anyone who knew Marion at all was aware such a statement had no merit. The power of conviction that Marion could hold to was always rooted in love.

The gist of the article was about Marion selling herself out to Robert Bly who the unnamed sources characterized as a charlatan and chauvinist. The author does quote an American feminist, Ann Jones, who saw Marion as being naïve in partnering with someone who wants to return to nature and get in touch with the natural, wild man inside.

Over the years, Marion gave several talks in Toronto, often at the University of Toronto. Each time the crowd was bigger than the last. I recall one snowy night in February, the large main auditorium at the Ontario Institute for Studies in Education was full and people were lined up, all the way down Bloor Street, disgruntled because they could not get in. Bigger and bigger venues had to be sought for her talks and this continued right up to November 2009, the last formal talk she gave at the University of Toronto. Ross told me how the same phenomena happened in London, England, where they prepared for an audience of 100 and 800 showed up. The same happened in the United States and in South America. What was behind this attraction could be puzzling, because her talks challenged people both psychologically and spiritually. According to this article, University of Toronto English professor, Robertson Davies, had an explanation. "Marion is an enchantress, who amorously solicits her female audience and puts a spell on them."[11] This accusation seemed like something right out of the witch trials! The ability to cast spells on women had to be the reason for these large audiences, even though at least one-third of the audience were men and many of the women were very accomplished, even formidable, hardly the type to be spellbound. Such critics can,

[11] Ibid., p. 81.

perhaps, be forgiven for not understanding that Marion spoke authentically from a deep heart place within, and in so doing awakened the soul in her audience. Even if her audience did not know what happened, they knew something had happened.

Often, pausing to enter a room, Marion would be quiet and composed. Then suddenly there was a presence that flowed through her to everyone around. It is not a case of summoning her persona but rather, an opening to the transparent honesty that characterized her life. She became charismatic, a fact she could acknowledge, but particularly in the beginning, was equally baffled by, as well as the large crowds she would attract. I remember teasing her about her charisma, but the reality can be found in the Oxford Dictionary which defines charisma as "a divinely conferred power or talent." While such a gift can be used for good or ill, I remember a word of wisdom once passed on to Marion and she passed on to me: "Before you stand in front of a group of people, recollect your soul and remember you are a woman greatly loved and capable of great loving." The energy you give is the energy you will get back. Given the effect on the audience and their awakened thirst for self-knowledge, it seems to me, this definition of charisma describes exactly one of the gifts Marion needed to carry out her unique destiny.

Not to leave Bly out of the equation, Davies also made the point that he would never be caught "dancing away his shadow."[12] Clearly, Dionysus would not be welcome here, except, perhaps, in his repressed and destructive form. What brought this article to mind was the condemnation of the wild man, the repressed natural energy that wants, and needs, to come into our culture. Seen from the perspective of twenty years, I think the article can be dismissed as written by someone who confused feminism with conscious femininity and had not embraced the hidden dynamics of the psyche. Like the Dark Goddess, it is an example of the degree of repression the Dark Stranger, the natural/wild man suffers in our culture and why. As an archetypal constellation, he is only now coming into consciousness.

---

[12] Ibid., p. 81.

Whatever one might think of Robert Bly or his poetry, he was in touch with a very real archetypal energy in our psyche that needs to become conscious. He, plus James Hillman and Michael Meade, gave many workshops for men putting them in touch with the natural man inside and their ability to express this energy in creative ways. The title of their workshops, "Men and the Life of Desire;" was exactly what I was observing. Consciously cut off from our true instinct for life, the wild man often finds his way into our culture through alcohol, drugs, and violence, particularly against women. If unrecognized, Dionysian energy can lead to madness. It is interesting that one of the major critics of Bly's work at that time was a well-known distillery. Their advertising message to men was clear: why hug a tree when real masculine virility is in a bottle.

The looming cancer diagnosis along with this misguided little challenge to Marion's insight and integrity were all part of a darkness that gave way to the light in the following year. Not only was there a reprieve from the cancer but, interestingly, there was a second article written a month following the release of *Dancing in the Flames*. It appeared in Maclean's, a popular Canadian magazine with widespread distribution. Entitled "A Midwife of Souls," it was written by journalist, Marci McDonald. This article starts with the unusual introduction and Convocation address at Western University given by Marion on receiving one of her three honorary doctorates. Having been there, I could relive the occasion through McDonald's words. Like any good journalist, Marci not only attended Marion's Investiture but also a workshop with her and Robert, who had enormous respect for Marion as expressed in a poem he wrote about her, "The Woman Who Knows." The controversy surrounding her association with Bly was addressed by MacDonald, including an interview with Bly and the observations of Ann Petrie, the well-known broadcaster involved in the filming of the six-part television series, "Bly and Woodman on Men and Women."

The controversy began in 1987 when Bly invited Marion to a Great Mother Conference. In McDonald's words, "When he [Bly] introduced her with a damning indictment of Jungian jargon a few in the audience were horrified by what they saw as his bullying. Woodman repaired to her hotel room to rewrite her speech, delivering it with only one stroke of puckish defiance. Now, that incident has become the running gag in a partnership immortalized in their 1991 television series, and director Ann Petrie still chuckles over the 'kind of Tracy-Hepburn banter in their dialogue.'...To watch them together, most recently in New York City last month, their delight in each other's company is obvious. 'I look over at her in amazement and she's saying things I've never thought of, Bly says.'... But feminists accuse Woodman of consorting with the enemy. It is an impression she flatly rejects. 'I say what I need to say...and when I need more space, I tell him to hold his top.'"[13]

Not content with anonymous sources, McDonald sought out insightful people who knew Marion well. One of those, author Jean Houston, spoke to the dynamic underlying Marion's work: "Marion is the bridge builder between the male and female worlds. She's one of the few people who understand that dynamic."[14]

My reason for bringing up these articles is twofold. The first article clearly shows our culture's repression and fear of this "wild" energy, not only among the older members of academia but in the larger population. Repressed, this energy can come out in all manner of addictions; or if overly identified with, such wild energy can be seen in the anarchy and terror so prevalent in much of the world today. If such energy remains unconscious it will ultimately blow itself up and everything around it.

Secondly, the deepest insight I had about the relationship between Marion and Robert came when I realized that *while I was collecting my clients' dreams about the "wild" man, Marion had stepped into the role of dealing with him.* I don't think she realized

---

[13] McDonald, Marci. (May 13, 1996). A Midwife of Souls. *Maclean's,* 61.
[14] Ibid., p. 58.

this but, in a very real sense, she *was* a container for the wild man to come into our culture. First contact may be rough but with a strong, conscious feminine container the vital and creative energy represented by the wild man becomes a dance. Their relationship may seem controversial to some, but it was a fascinating and creative relationship in view of our current culture that still prefers its self-defeating addictions as a substitute for the ecstatic wild man.

I realize that the workshops in which Marion and Robert tried to bring both men and women to the still point are a living record of this need for integration. Still, I wonder if a written record of dreams, encounters, and reflections with the wild man energy might have served a purpose. Of course, everything that is meant to be will come around again.

The wild man is the 2,000,000-year-old man in all of us. He is at the very beginning of recorded history and the beginning of the patriarchal paradigm. Enkidu, the wild man, challenged the king Gilgamesh for his grandiosity and the treatment of his people, particularly the treatment of women. A dream had foretold that Gilgamesh and Enkidu *together* would do great things, but Enkidu, on entering the city, was eventually overpowered by the archetypal energy of the king. The Goddess was denigrated, the spirit of Nature killed, and Enkidu had to die, falling back into the unconscious where he has remained. In Greek mythology, while Dionysus was faithful to one woman, Apollo, the god of light and reason, turned women into trees or robbed them of their voice. While feminists such as Ann Jones may fear the wild man, they fail to realize that without his return, women will never be able to take their rightful place. In the Grail story, it is not the fair-haired Sir Lancelot but the dark-haired Gawain who knows the sovereign place of the feminine, the world of deep connection and flow able to restore the wasteland.

Dionysus riding on a cheetah. Public Domain, via Wikimedia Commons.

ELEVEN

[Our] relationship to the patterns in our bodies is as important as our relationship to the patterns in our psyches.

Marion

One of the many things I learned from Marion was a deeper appreciation of the implications of the psychoid archetype. Archetypes are not visible in themselves, but as the new metaphors of science might suggest, they are patterns of active information in the quantum plenum. Initially Jung saw the archetypal image as the instinct's perception of itself, or the self-portrait of the instinct very much rooted in the body. As his understanding grew, Jung finally came to the realization of archetypes as mediating factors of the *unus mundus*. As such, he understood that the same archetype operated simultaneously in both the realms of psyche and matter. As psyche they are dynamical organizers of images, and when operating in the realm of matter, they are the patterning principles of energy. This has become more understandable now that science has realized the acausal order within the physical world and provides structuring principles for causal processes. The more conscious we become, the more aware we are of the occurrence of synchronistic phenomena. In the process of coming to wholeness, we become aware that the patterns in our bodies and the patterns in our psyche both have to be acknowledged to bring us into a harmonious relationship within ourselves. Meeting someone like Marion, who understood so deeply the dynamic of making the unconscious conscious through working with the patterns at both ends of the spectrum, was a fundamental help in allowing me to grasp what was going on, not only within me, but with my clients.

One evening I went over to Marion's clutching a new book in my hand: Candace Pert's *Molecules of Emotion*. I arrived to learn that someone had just given a copy to Marion. These pages not only contain a further validation that psyche and soma are one, but the necessity of working with both simultaneously. Pert's pioneering work with neuropeptides led her to conclude that:

> The mind is in the flow of information as it moves among the cells, organs, and systems of the body. And since one of the qualities of information flow is that it can be un-conscious, occurring below the level of awareness, we see it in operation at the automatic, or involuntary, level of our physiology. The mind as we experience it is immaterial, yet it has a physical substrate, which is both body and the brain. It may also be said to have a nonmaterial, non-physical substrate that has to do with the flow of that information. The mind, then, is that which holds the network together, often acting below our consciousness, linking and coordinating the major systems and their organs and cells in an in-telligently orchestrated symphony of life. Thus, we might refer to the whole system as a psychosomatic information network, linking *psyche*, which comprises all that is of an ostensibly immaterial nature, such as mind, emotion, and soul, to *soma*, which is the material world of molecules, cells, and organs. Mind and body, psyche and soma.[15]

---

[15] Pert, Candace. (1997). *Molecules of Emotion* (p. 185). New York, New York: Simon & Schuster.

Seeing the body as the unconscious mind, Pert realized that repressed traumas due to overwhelming emotion become stored in the body and can affect our perception. Releasing these repressed traumas in the body was the focus of Marion's body/soul work and the results can often be seen in dream imagery in which plugged toilets are able to flush; broken down cars are able to run again; new rooms are discovered in old houses; electrical wiring is repaired, or crippled animals are healed. Our own energy was flowing that night as we each enthusiastically shared the highlighted sections of our individual copy of Pert's book.

Conversations with Marion, along with my own experience and the gift of dreams from my clients formed much of our discussions during the late '80s and '90s. While she was uncovering a wealth of knowledge working through body/soul intensives, through dream work and active imagination expressed in masks and movement, I would bring my own thoughts and what I was learning through working with my clients. In the dreams of my clients, for example, I became aware that the patterns often presented themselves with great clarity:

> *A man dreams about going into an unknown large stone house. He wanders around and finally is drawn down into the basement. He keeps going down and down until he comes to a place where he finds a young girl of five or six crouched in the corner. He is heartbroken to see the girl bound with yellow strands, like long ties for tying up garbage, criss-crossing her body. He decides he must loosen them, one tie at a time.*

Similarly, a woman had three dreams, each one a regression in age:

In the third dream she comes to her five-year-old daughter who is having a playful time taking her dog out for a walk. Suddenly the leash becomes yards of twine in which the little girl and her dog become totally tied up. The girl is almost dead, but the dreamer manages to unravel all the twine from her body just in time to revive her.

These dreams, one from a man and one from a woman, show the young feminine soul being bound and tossed aside or strangled by the age of five or six, the age when we enter the school system or are expected to behave in a certain way. The creative life is often choked out of us. In the case of the man, the yellow ribbons seem to correspond to the third chakra which breaks the flow of feelings from reaching the heart. For many people the energy is cut off at an early age limiting us to the scripts and platitudes of family and culture. Ideologies become prisons preventing the creative imagination from envisioning anything new. From Marion's viewpoint, when we are programmed to society's norms, particularly those based in patriarchal values, anyone who sets out to become a unique individual trusting in their instincts and the creativity of their imagination runs the risk of becoming an outcast.

The frequency of habitual thoughts in the mind correlates with the energy patterns set up in the body. Such patterns, often fixed to support ideals, subvert the instinct for life into the instinct for death. Only when we can allow our instincts to reveal their deep, embodied wisdom, the forgotten wisdom of Sophia, can we, and the planet, move toward life. Our dreams may point to our repressed vitality for life, but we usually need ritual: art, music, and dance to release them and let the energy flow.

Addictions, by definition, are all the patterns that keep us paralyzed or caught in self-repeating, destructive patterns. After Marion, we can never look at addictions in the same way again. In having to wrestle with her own demon, the gift that Marion received for the psychological and spiritual growth of many people was the necessity of working with the body. We can have conscious insight into what our trauma may be, but if the body does not find a way of letting go of the trauma, our actions will be crippled. The recognition of these destructive patterns, their release and subsequent transformation, formed the core of Marion's work. This work would grow not only in the numbers of people who resonated with its energy, but psychically, as people engaged in working with whatever complexes and patterns hindered the release of soul and spirit into the world. The inner marriage of mature feminine and masculine energies is the treasure awaiting those who engage in this demanding work.

Deep resonance and an upsurge of energy and inspiration is a sure sign of Sophia erupting into our consciousness. This enthusiastic resonance surfaced one evening in the late 1990s, as I read Brian Bates book, *The Way of Wyrd*, based, in part, on pre-Christian documents in the British Museum, along with other historical documents of the time. As a multi-dimensional cosmic web, the archetypal worldview that Wyrd presents draws us into a way of living in touch with nature and the spiritual dimension. The worldview of my ancestors not only supported Jung and quantum physics but also the analytic process that many of my clients were going through today. Gathering all these threads, I wrote an unpublished essay called "The Cauldron," partly as a way of exploring my own Indigenous roots and their relevance for today.

Bates presents his research in the story of an Anglo-Saxon sorcerer, called Wulf, and his young Christian initiate, called Brand. In Brand's attempt to understand the Indigenous people he is meant to serve, he discovers his own soul. One of the first steps in his initiation requires old patterns in the body to be loosened. In this tale, Brand is attacked by a swarm of bees leaving him covered with a mass of small red swellings concentrated across the stomach, merging into one great streak of red like an open wound on his side. Addressing him, the sorcerer says, "The Wyrd Sisters have loosened your fibres. Your fibres can now move freely according to the tides and currents of

Wyrd, the positions of the stars, the pattern of the sun and moon and the most insignificant of distant events."[16] For my Indigenous ancestors, the body was not a machine with defined boundaries and functions; it was connected to the earth and the cosmos, the playground of the soul.

Many people have their own bee experience—an accident, cancer, or the death of a loved one—that opens them to seek a greater dimension and depth in life. This, of course, is only the first step. For new life to arise out of the chaos, our ancestors understood that an increase in life force was necessary. The herb spearwort was used to increase the life force, but it is very dangerous and requires elaborate preparations—a secret known to Anglo-Saxon sorcerers. In this tale the sorcerer Wulf says, "Spearwort will vastly increase your inner fire. And when you sit between two wildfires, you enter a vast cauldron of forces flowing through you like the wind. Changes in power within you are reflected by changes outside you, for all the patterns of Wyrd are present in the body in the same way as they are present in the sun, moon, and stars."[17] That is, the release of blocked energy in the body results in an increased passion for life. Once you are open to the vibrations of the world around you, you can begin to live in harmony with their creative forces.

The soul can begin to guide you from within through the power of dreams. In Wulf's words, "Waking life wallows in the indulgences of the word-hoard. Words spin webs of deception and delusion. They shape and falsify our experience of Wyrd to serve the human masters of fear and vanity."[18] This is a sentiment we can still relate to in 2018, a period that has been recognized as a time of post-truth. In dreams, however, we meet the truth; the true images that reveal the hidden aspects of our Being. As Wulf instructs Brand, "in dreams, the things we meet, even our enemies, tell us the truth, for in dreams we meet souls freed from the fears and foibles of Middle-Earth. Dreams offer

---

[16] Bates, Brian. (1983). The Way of Wyrd: Tales of an Anglo-Saxon Sorcerer, (p.126) San Francisco, CA, *Harper*.
[17] Ibid. p. 160.
[18] Ibid., p. 160

a fragmentary glimpse of the spirit-world. To enter the sorcery of Wyrd one needs only to dream."[19]

Anna Gormley is a very talented body/energy therapist, and together we decided to do some weekend workshops using a therapeutic template related to our roots. Often, Greek mythology or fairy tales are used as containers to explore the psyche, but we decided to use this Anglo-Saxon tale as a base. Woundedness is always a place to start, because it is, so often, the recognition of the wound that allows for healing to begin. Secondly, not knowing the secret of spearwort, we had to work with first-chakra energy as well as with breathing, meditation, and dance, always mindful of the images and dreams that came from the unconscious. These were the images we worked with, in our bodies (from Marion) and then recorded our experience. At the beginning and at the end of the workshop we scanned the body. Comparing the early trauma with the locked-down patterns in the first, versus the last, body scanning showed marked differences, which led to further discussions and dreams that were followed in analysis.

The initiate, Brand, continued his journey involving sacred places, sacred geometry, and above all, sound and movement. He had to be able to sing his own song, to know his own voice. As his body became more ensouled, he finally encountered the world-soul, who had been there all along but was now consciously realized. For me, this was a marvelous tale that I could associate with my own introduction to the dream world. Wyrd speaks to an integral worldview before the advent of the split, material world we find ourselves in today, before the 16th century when we wandered into the cave of Medusa and she turned us into stone.

It could be said that Anna and I were engaged in a 9th century version of body/soul rhythms, from a time before we thought of ourselves as machines. This is the kind of fun-filled creative tension Marion and I shared, such as comparing this ancient initiation, coming

---

[19] Ibid., pp. 170-171.

from our common Indigenous roots to some of the experiences and goals of the Body/Soul Rhythm workshops she was offering.

Another process that affirmed the advantage of working directly with the body came from my client, Anne. Her earlier dream (page 82) tells of the Black Goddess leading her into the center of the crystal mandala. With consent, Anne's journey became a case study of psyche/soma integration that Beverly Stokes and I presented at the Sheraton Hotel in downtown Toronto at an International Movement and Psychotherapy Meeting. Earlier, Marion had introduced me to Beverly, who did a form of bodywork based on human development patterns and evolutionary origins. Working with Beverly, Ann began to have dreams that went right to the molecular level. In one such dream she is floundering in deep water with ugly crocodile creatures surrounding her. She tried everything to get away, but they were always there. Defiantly, she started screaming, "Eat me, just eat me! Come on, I don't care!" Once confronted, the crocodiles suddenly change into neon-tetra (tiny, rainbow-colored, tropical fish). "There are thousands of them and they are swimming all around me. As we come up from the deep water, the sun is reflecting off them revealing dazzling colors. Gleefully, I try to gather armfuls of them as I come up out of the water."

This dream clarifies what happens in the unconscious when blocks are removed from energy channels in the body. It is an example of what Jung calls *enantiodromia*, the reversal of a psychic situation. The crocodiles, the chthonic mother, is not about to let the dream ego escape. They have been concretized in her body for a long time. No matter how she twists and turns there is no way out. She does not give up but in the face of a supernatural challenge stops fighting and surrenders, "Just eat me!" By exposing her vulnerability, she transforms the menacing energy that pulls toward death into energy vibrant with light. The Death Goddess shifts into Life Goddess. The body is no longer concretized in fear. The very cells of the body are loosened from the grip of fear and explode into vibrant multi-colored carriers of life.

When Anne came to see me nine months earlier, I administered the Rorschach test, partly to convince her that her colleagues at the

University were right to be worried about her. Having been struck by the power of her dreams, I administered the test again at the end of her analysis. The results showed a significant drop in the intellectualization score which represents a major way in which the individual organizes his or her perceptions of the world. For Anne, intellectualization was a major part of her defensive posture and is highly resistant to change, no matter what the intervention. By letting go of her need to control through rational means, her emotions began to surface. Rage and loneliness became much more evident in her profile. With the surfacing of these emotions, her psychic discomfort also rose. The test showed that Anne's perception had moved from external scanning to internal scanning. She had previously manifested a defensive posture toward the world, overly alert to what was happening "out there." Now, she could look more inward for the answers and cues, within herself. Her subsequent dreams show that she was now ready to begin working gradually towards achieving a new balance between spirit and matter, Eros and Logos.

Trained in the scientific method, I could ask, "Would that depth of transformation in such a relatively short period have been possible without the bodywork?" There is no objective way of knowing, but common sense and my own experience would say, "No!" Human movement is rooted in our evolutionary inheritance and forms the early patterns we learn and develop as infants. The work Beverly[20] does in re-sequencing these early patterns can open a greater depth of physical and psychic experience. When these subcortical centers are engaged, the dreams often show the transformation taking place in vivid, startling forms. The prismatic reflections of the body of light known as the rainbow body in Tibet Buddhism, become apparent at the cellular level when the crocodiles become tiny, rainbow-colored fish. Similarly, in another dream Anne is asked to slough off the skin of a snake, revealing the same rainbow-colored body underneath. The snake "winks" and thanks her profusely. Her deepest instincts are

---

[20] Beverly Stokes trained with Bonnie Bainbridge Cohen in developmental processes and experiential anatomy.

released into life. Anne dreams of putting on all kinds of diving, breathing gear as defenses before she goes into the ocean, the unconscious depths. Transformation comes when she takes off all her artificial gear and swims, like a newborn, in the watery depths. Working with Beverly on the post-natal, and probably pre-natal, developmental structures in the body, Anne was able to restore a new harmonic balance symbolized by riding the dolphin who is now guiding her through the waves. The deep developmental bodywork that Anne did with Beverly was essential in Anne's radical journey. Of course, I would never have been open to that possibility if it were not for Marion's work.

While Marion and her colleagues were gaining more and deeper insight into the dynamic interchange between psyche/soma, I was often led into my own explorations. This was not by design; it just seemed to happen that way but in the tapestry of our friendship there were many nodule points that held the warp and woof together. When we got together, we often shared the experiences or insights we had unearthed. Often these conversations lead to not only articulating the transformation happening "out there" but, given the level of trust between us, the transformations happening within. Particularly at a time when Marion was receiving some criticism of her work, including from other analysts, I think we both gained affirmation and support through our seemingly parallel journeys. Each standing in our own truth, Sophia worked synchronistically in and through us in different ways. I began to realize it was the parallel yet complementary nature of our relationship that so often provided the excitement in the ongoing, deepening discovery of where we were being led.

Dealing with the patterns in our body/soul on a more personal level, Marion often commented that she possessed a Jaguar engine in a Volkswagen chassis that could often throw her process out of balance. Early on, she realized that her spiritual energy was beyond her body's capacity to embody it. This phenomenon was a reality we both struggled with and underlines how important Marion was in guiding me into the necessity of releasing old patterns in the body for spirit and soul to unite. Intense spiritual energy can throw the body off balance.

For almost 30 years I suffered from what doctors called a spastic colon. They could draw pictures of what it looked like, but they couldn't do anything except stop the peristalsis, which doesn't really work. Never knowing when it was going to strike could, at times, leave me living on the edge. For the last 30-plus years I have been totally cured. My symptoms started with the intensity of my spiritual desire and ended through a unique combination of body/soul work.

While doing bodywork with John Went to release the old patterns and traumas, I met a Chinese medicine practitioner whom I invited to come to the hospital to teach Tai Chi to the psychology staff. In discussing my personal plight, I was told my Chi was out of balance, the energy channels were blocked by certain patterns in the body. For an hour a day, over eight consecutive days, I was gently but powerfully worked on, with only the use of finger tips. I could feel the energy going into my body. I believe the engagement of both psyche and soma, releasing the energy contained in my dreams and opening the energy channels in my body, allowed the intense spiritual energy to finally come in unimpeded.

The great mystics, Teresa of Avila and John of the Cross experienced the same phenomena. In the 16th century, John of the Cross expressed it this way: "As, however, this sensual part of the soul is weak and incapable of experiencing the strong things of the spirit, it follows that these proficients, by reason of this spiritual communication which is made to their sensual part, endure therein many frailties and sufferings and weaknesses of the stomach, and in consequence are fatigued in spirit."[21]

Similarly, in his seminars on Zarathustra, Jung states that the body, if it remains unconscious, cannot absorb the psychic pressure imposed upon it, which can cause the mind to snap. Jung felt it was this inability to sustain the psychic pressure that occasioned Nietzsche's psychotic break. Reading Jung's Zarathustra lectures,

---

[21] Marie-Eugene, P. (1955). *I am a Daughter of the Church* (p. 337). Chicago: Fides Publishers.

Marion gained a deep understanding that one must be able to release the destructive patterns in both mind and body to weave the spiritual womb capable of holding the transformative power that connects body, soul, and spirit.

Sitting at the crossroads, our imaginary meeting place, Marion and I, coming from different directions, could share insights that enriched us both. Marion opened the archetypal world to me, and ever since I have been "travelling along my fibres," going to those places where my heart burned within me, gaining more and more insight into soul. I know from things she said over the years that many times I held that same space for her.

TWELVE

In describing the continual creation and destruction of
particles as a rhythmic dance, physicists are describing the
Black Goddess. The rhythm of death and life, chaos and
creativity, is symbolized in the dance of Kali, a dance in
which we are invited to take part.

Marion

In the early '90s, Marion attended a Conference on Chaos Theory
at the University of Toronto. It was one of those synchronistic
occurrences, insofar as I had taken the summer of that same year to
immerse myself in a self-study of Chaos Theory. Without consulting
each other, it seems we both had the idea to explore chaos as the
necessary vortex of the ongoing creativity of the soul. You cannot
enter the irrational world of the feminine, nature, or the dark god,
without encountering the process of chaos. As I quoted earlier, even
after the cancer diagnosis was rendered null and void, Marion still felt
there was a deeper cycle of chaos/creation out there that she had to
move into. Her reflections formed part of a chapter in *Dancing in the
Flames* entitled "Chaos and Creativity."

Interest in chaos and chaos theory has deep roots in Jung. In fact,
it is fundamental to his understanding of psyche and the process of
individuation. This premise became abundantly clear in the recently
published *The Red Book*. Jung writes: "There in the world of chaos

dwells eternal wonder...Man belongs not only to an ordered world, he also belongs to the wonder-world of his soul."[22] That is, the soul as the creative matrix is essentially chaotic. Entering more deeply into this chaos, Jung writes: "Everything inside me is in utter disarray. Matters are becoming serious, and chaos is approaching. Is this the ultimate bottom? Is chaos also a foundation? If only there weren't these terrible waves. Everything breaks asunder like black billows."[23] Encountering chaos is essential for individuation, because the unconscious itself, the place of transformation, is chaotic. But what Jung found in his descent into chaos is that if one is open to it, "magic also arises." The key words are "if one is open to it." The degree of openness to the transformative magic implied in that statement depends on the health and flexibility of the ego that can withstand the onslaught of the chaotic forces and consciously surrender to them, allowing something new to emerge.

While the patterns may be loosened, from the ego's perspective it is always an experience of death. Death, physical or psychical, that leads to life depends on whether the ego is healthy enough to surrender—to open to the magic of transformation, a resurrection into something new. From the viewpoint of soul, death isn't really the opposite of life; it is the opposite of birth, including rebirth. The deeper we are called into life the more we must confront death.

Earlier (p.23) I related my actual confrontation with death in 1979 in Africa. A second confrontation came in the form of an unattended burst appendix. For two days I was in agonizing pain with a high fever. At one point, at the foot of my bed stood two large figures (more like pure energy), one light and the other dark. I saw them as life and death. While I was focusing on life I realized, and what has stayed with me, is that in the end, death is the friend who releases us into the infinite. I cannot say I have any fondness for pain, but death became much less fearful. Suddenly the pain stopped, and I was grateful. I crawled from my bed into an adjoining washroom only to discover

---

[22] Jung, Carl. (2009). *The Red Book* (p. 264). New York and London: W. W. Norton and Company.
[23] Ibid., p. 298.

that my chest and joints were oozing pus. I was too weak to even shower. I returned to bed and slept for twenty-four hours. The next day I could get up and venture out to find food. Returning to the hospital a week later, X-rays showed only a scar where the appendix should be. They couldn't quite figure out how I was alive. With that much poison circulating in my system, some of it must have been dumped into the colon as well as coming out through the skin. Apparently, few people live through such an ordeal, so they didn't know what to advise me except not to travel to places that didn't have good medical facilities!

As Marion stated on several occasions, she learned everything through the body, so it was not surprising that she underwent several life/death/rebirth experiences. We die into life or we die into death. The addictive world we live in today is a dying into death. Marion has talked and written so profoundly about this on many occasions. Are we dying into death or are we dying into life? The touchstone, it seems to me, is whether we can escape our unconscious repetitive patterns by surrendering the ego's control to a point that allows the life-giving love to flow through us.

As a repetitive pattern, anorexia was Marion's first encounter with death unto death. She was 27 when her addictive illness led her to death's door. This was a hitting-the-bottom experience of many addicts but it carried with it a cry for life. Desperately choosing life is, in my own experience, a cry that does not go unheeded by Sophia. At 18, alone and broke and 3,000 miles from home, I had reached a point where I thought I couldn't go on. Falling on my knees and choosing life with its attendant surrender resulted later that year in a scholarship to attend a prestigious university as a resident. Marion's way came more slowly but it came.

For Marion, another early confrontation with death came in the form of a car accident that left her badly injured, particularly on one side of her face. She was always grateful to the plastic surgeon for his remarkable restoration. The only trace is a slight drooping of the eye when she is overtired. The other symptom she was left with was the persistent ringing in her ears. As written about earlier, this condition would lead to one of her most life-changing encounters with the Self; an encounter with Sophia in which she recognized the depths to which she was loved.

India, perhaps, became Marion's major place of life-changing chaos. The Western minister's daughter and English teacher suddenly found herself in a world that pulsed with its own, seemingly chaotic, rhythm. In going to India, the initial plan included meeting up with a friend and going to an ashram. Upon her arrival, these initial arrangements fell through, and Marion found herself alone in a city teaming with life but also with poverty and disease. The extreme cultural shock and dysentery resulted in a near-death experience. As so often happens, such chaos precedes the emergence of some totally new realization, if we can consciously surrender. Marion wept for her body and in so doing allowed the love of Sophia to flow through her. As she clung to the abyss, a large, dark-skinned woman came to sit with her in the hotel lobby and through the warmth emanating from her body slowly brought Marion back to life. As she often said, the God she once worshipped turned out to be a She in India.

Sometimes there is a time or a place that is pivotal in our life. India was that time and place for Marion. It was a time when she remembered that she had a Goddess. Through her surrender, Marion began to see life as incarnation, as embodiment, but more importantly, she began to understand that love is stronger than death. This realization allows us to surrender and carries us through from individuation to realization.

Marion's more recent confrontation with death began in 1993 in her battle with cancer. In experiencing the soul's process, we continually spiral higher and deeper, and this understanding was the background when, in 2000, she wrote *Bone: Dying into Life,* a profound reflection on the role cancer played in her journey. While in the past she had taken her body and Nature for granted, over the years she had come to a much deeper realization of both. This time, her confrontation with death would lead her to really *experience* the

124

sacredness of matter, the immanent light of Sophia, in a more embodied way. Her reflections took her back to India and the Black Madonna that she now embraced as the life force of Nature itself in all its nurturing and passionate energy. I remember sitting with her on the rocky shore of Georgian Bay, looking at a flower growing out of the cracks in the rock. She spoke of her body as the rejected stone, not recognized as sacred, and yet from within it, the life force could break through. Her reflections in *Bone* end with her ability to enter a deeper, more conscious, wild feminine energy that can dance into life—and death.

In the 40 years after India, Marion went through many spirals of life, death, and rebirth, each time surrendering to the creative matrix of the body. Each time, new treasures arose from the depths.

Order and chaos are interconnected sides of the same coin. We undergo many deaths in our lifetime. We need such experiences to grow, to let old patterns die so new ones can emerge. Particularly since the Great Plague of the 14th century, when we were universally traumatized by irrational death, our culture over the last 500 years

Wildflowers growing out of rock, Sha Sha Island, 1991.

has sought to shut out chaos through rational control, reductionism, and fundamentalism. We need a deeper grasp and appreciation of the role of chaos, personally and culturally, to once more embrace the evolutionary, *transformative* cycles of life, death, and rebirth. If we enter consciously into the process of chaos, we can restore our deep connection with Nature and the World Soul.

As within, so without! In the past 25 years, chaos theory has also shaken up the scientific world and loosened a few patterns. Before the advent of scientific materialism, order and chaos were both acknowledged, even if there was an uneasy tension between them. The drive for order, resulting in reductionism and determinism, built up a one-sided energy that would unconsciously be released, and the pendulum would have to swing to the other side. Following the devastating wars of the 20th century, scientists suddenly (re)discovered chaos. I don't think it is a coincidence that this happened at a time when the world was falling apart. When scientists studying chaos famously found that a butterfly flapping its wings in Mexico can cause a tornado in Kansas just as the shot that killed Archduke Ferdinand started a world war. When we scientifically track chaotic systems, we find there is not only a destructive descent into chaos, but, that chaos contains an inner dynamic that leads to the possibility of further creativity and a new wholeness. Hopefully, even in political chaos of today, new green shoots can grow through the rubble.

Researchers such as Ilya Prigogine began to view nature not as a hierarchical structure but as a dynamical, shifting web. By the 1950s, the orderly world of determinism was being challenged on multiple sides. By 1977, the Academy of Sciences held a symposium on chaos in New York with scientists such as David Ruelle, Robert May, and James Yorke. Ruelle was among the first to make the comparison between strange attractors and archetypes. The magnetic quality of attractors organized around "missing information" began to form a new order out of chaos. Early on, Jung recognized that chaos has its own implicit order—different from the simple causal order we are conditioned to.

Order to chaos to order, science has rediscovered the great rhythm of nature—life, death, and rebirth. A new mathematics of fractals demonstrating holographic iterative processes going to infinity arose to meet this emerging understanding of reality. As researchers began to trace the order arising from chaos, the new science of complexity and non-linear dynamical self-organizing systems was born. For those who knew Jung's work, it became very apparent that he had discovered the dynamics of complexity early on. As in many areas he now had the findings of science to affirm his discoveries.

The discoveries on the scientific front are now affirming the degree of accuracy Jung attained in his observations and experience of *how* the psyche works. More importantly, we are beginning to realize that we live in one world, the dynamic patterns behind matter and psyche emerging from a unitary source. Those who have worked with chaos in their own lives and in their own bodies know this seemingly disruptive process contains the potential for new life emerging, as it does, from the underlying dynamic of Soul—if we can consciously surrender to the process.

At 18, Marion exchanged the poetry she found at the end of a microscope for the poetry she found in literature. But it was poetry, nonetheless. A metaphor is not only transitional, changing one thing into another, but a metaphor implies nuance implicit in the margins that engage our imagination, feeling, and capacity for meaning. Metaphors open us to new dimensions. In the words of John Briggs and F. David Peat, "The poet unfolding nuance is like an equation iterating on the boundary between finite order and infinite chaos."[24]

---

[24] Briggs, John & Peat, F. David. (1989). *Turbulent Mirror* (p. 195). New York, New York: Harper & Rowe.

In Marion's work, poetry and science were coming together once more.

At 40, I experienced going beyond time and space and becoming one with a single, universal vibration of Love. So, when I read statements like: "The world we see might be the manifestation of a single iterative self-referential process,"[25] or "From the iterative reciprocal relating perspective, it is easy to imagine that the universe is one huge completely interconnected process"[26]—I get it

[25] May, Josephine & Martin Groder, "Jungian Thought and Dynamical Systers," *in Psychological Perspectives*, Spring-Summer, 1989, Vol. 20, #1, p. 152.
[26] Ibid., p. 152.

THIRTEEN

Jung foresaw intuitively what the connections were going to be between body and mind and mind and spirit. I'm interested in scientific research that will look into many of his intuitive insights about medicine and the mind-body connection.

Marion

The deeper we go into the inner world, the more we recognize ourselves in the outer world. The energy released within, once it becomes conscious, flows out, mirroring the world around us. Through both our journeys, Marion and I were destined to explore the interface between spirit and matter. At this time in history, such a pursuit cannot bypass science. As biology, physics, and cosmology probe more deeply into the heart of matter they uncover the archetypal dimensions of our psyches from which science, like art, arises.

In her university studies, Marion balanced her deep interest in biology with English literature. Given her brilliant mind, a career as a researcher in the biological sciences would, no doubt, have been successful. Aware of the expressive need of her neglected feeling, she made the decision to enroll in university primarily as a student of literature. Having moved through the depths of image and metaphor, feminine consciousness, and the light in nature, the wheel has come full circle. With an inner masculine, now capable of articulating nature with a thinking heart, Marion's love of science once more became an arena where the mysteries of the sacred feminine were being revealed.

Never having lost her passion for science, even in her earliest talks and writing, Marion delighted in weaving the insights of quantum physics and the new biology into her understanding of the psyche. This passion would find a direct expression in two keynote addresses to the Noetics Society and a lecture at the Smithsonian. Three different articles were published in the magazine Caduceus, published in the United Kingdom. Eager for a more lasting format for the science of psyche and soma, she established the Marion Woodman Scholarship Fund at California's Pacifica Graduate Institute: Depth Psychology specialization in the Somatic Studies Program. In 1999, Marion made a large donation to New College, University of Toronto, to create the Marion Woodman Legacy Fund. In 2005, Marion and her husband Ross jointly established a scholarship fund for two students each year interested in interdisciplinary studies in Jungian psychology. Marion chose New College because of its commitment to fostering the union of science and the humanities. She was convinced that this was the perfect place for this research into the vision held by Jung and eagerly looked forward to interacting with psychiatrists, medical doctors, scientists, theologians and others at the speaker's series. The hope was that this series would encourage and give direction to the formal classes taught during the year.

The 1980s were an exciting time to delve into the new alchemy that science was unearthing. During this time, I met Julianna Switaj, then a Ph.D. student in psychology working on her doctoral thesis. Her previous training as a scientist, and her wonderful, agile, intuitive mind opened me to a whole new world. One day, Julianna showed up at my office with a copy of Danah Zohar's book, *The Quantum Body*. We spent several sessions after work at the whiteboard in a group/meeting room at St. Michael's discussing its implications. It was the first I learned of the reality of the *lumen naturae* in the work of Fritz Albert Popp who discovered biophotons (light) in our DNA.

In 1987, this led to Marion, Julianna and I meeting at Walmer Road for several very energetic discussions which we recorded and I volunteered to transpose to paper. On one occasion, we were talking of instincts and the natural order, and a common theme in dreams whereby animals are in the process of transforming into human beings. This transformation seems to imply instinctual matter permeated with light is becoming more subtle matter. The transcript of a typical conversation is as follows.

Marion: "Surrendering to the wholeness that comes from harmony with the natural order will make no sense to someone who is wedded to a Newtonian/Cartesian paradigm. Quantum physics, however, presents us with other possibilities."

Julianna: "Our very Beingness is the manifestation of energy patterns—a manifestation that is made up of many collapsed wave functions. The energy patterns of 'I' are whole themselves. It is only when 'I' clings to a part as if it were the whole that the energy patterns become disrupted. This can lead to a breakdown such as illness. Since it is the ego observer who creates a particular reality, to allow the energy patterns to reconfigure, we have to bypass the ordinary ego perceptions. The metaphor machine (from a dream image Marion was talking about earlier) is one way of doing this, because it acts as a bridge to the non-rational (non-dualistic) reality that we really are."

Marion: "Metaphor captures the passion, the movement, the meaning...If we focus the fire of our imagination, our own metaphors begin to heat and transform, opening up new energy channels in our body. In taking the imaginative leap, we embody the metaphor. In becoming the metaphor, we become whole. The wholeness may not last, but that moment rings like a tuning fork that the cells do not forget."[27]

Our discussions were far ranging, but with Marion becoming increasingly busy travelling and Julianna and her husband John moving to Guelph, these fun and enlightening discussions ended. I know

---

[27] Transcribed conversation partially presented in *Dancing in the Flames,* op. cit., pp. 191-192.

Marion was especially sorry to give them up. As our last meeting coincided with Marion's birthday, we had brought flowers and a small, decadent cake and three candles with which to celebrate. For us, meeting in person was always a celebration.

Although science did not dominate our conversation in the early days of our relationship, when I look back, it was a theme that increasingly became part of our shared interest. For both Marion and me, science was not some disembodied conceptual reality. Its importance lived at the heart of reality, and, therefore, at the heart of the psyche. From early on, I was aware that science, like all human endeavor, is essentially a spiritual discipline. In the 1979 weeklong workshop I gave with Thomas Berry (see pp.19-20) one of the things I remember was leading an ad hoc discussion on scientifically-based books as spiritual reading. At the time, I was reading Carl Sagan's *Dragons of Eden.* At this point in the workshop, most people in the room (a large contingent being women religious leaders) understood what I was getting at except for a very vociferous objection from the Jesuit Provincial who felt that seeing science from a spiritual perspective could lead us away from orthodox teaching.

For many years, usually on the 23rd, Marion and I celebrated Christmas together. One Christmas, as we were having dinner in front of the fireplace at Oliver's, our conversation, as usual, went from the personal to the transpersonal. That is, we talked about what was happening in our lives, how we felt about it, our health, the joys and challenges our families were facing, in short, a catching up on our personal agendas. Then the discussion turned to the images and metaphors in our dreams and their rootedness in the new science: a typical Christmas celebration—for us! "Elinor, as you read about quantum physics do you find similar images appearing in dreams?" "Yes," I replied, "I think the deeper we understand the relationship between psyche and soma the more this new imagery becomes apparent." During our discussion, I immediately thought of two dream images that affirmed our observation. My client Anne, who was so disembodied and cut off from her feelings, dreamed she was approaching a stage where colorfully dressed Chinese men were dancing and letting off firecrackers. Through them came a woman with a long flowing blue veil that billowed out at the dreamer. This was the energy, the flow that Anne needed in her life. She knew nothing about physics and we didn't allude to it, but I could see the unconscious with its precise, almost playful images speaking in the metaphors of particle and wave physics, a perfect image of particles popping in and out of the wave structure of reality. Particle and wave, masculine and feminine, order and chaos; our dreams can, and often do, reach back to the beginning of time.

Similarly, the dream of the large dark woman riding to shore on the crest of a wave, while she and her friends are all molecules in the wave, points to the prevalence of wave theory emerging in science. Every molecule has both a particle and wave function through which every molecule in the world is interconnected. Feminine energy is truly coming to shore. Molecules, dancing with the resonance of love, have their roots in the beginning of creation. We never took the time to explore in depth the deep underlying structure of dreams that science illuminates, but it must be there. Ultimately, there is only one reality.

My second brush with cancer in 2007, led me back into science through the new discipline of epigenetic medicine and the malleability of our DNA. Going through mounds of research on epigenetics and cancer, I became aware this was a breakthrough coming into consciousness that would cause many of Jung's critics, particularly in the 1950s, to fall by the wayside. While the biological aspect of Jung's archetypal theory never really depended on the work of the discredited naturalist, Jean Baptiste de Lamarck, he was criticized as being "too Lamarckian." Lamarck believed in the "inheritance of acquired traits" where the experiences acquired by one generation could be transmitted genetically to the next. Two hundred years ago, Lamarck was mocked, but now it seems he was largely right.

Motivated by the insights of epigenetics and the fact that the 60th anniversary of Jung's death would occur in 2011, I wanted to create my own tribute to him. To this end, I put together a yearlong course, "Jung in the 21st Century," based on interactions between Jung and today's cutting-edge scientists. Sonu Shamdasani gives us a remarkable history of Jung, outlining those who influenced him and those who criticized him. This would have to be the starting point on any comprehensive course on Jung. But the newly understood science of epigenetics prompted me to look to the present. As young men, Jung and Einstein dined together on several occasions. His later collaboration with the Nobel Laureate physicist Wolfgang Pauli is well known. If Jung were writing today, one might conclude that he was influenced by the research of David Bohm or theoretical physicist Laszlo Gazdag. Perhaps the work of physicist John Wheeler, Hal Puthoff or astrophysicist Bernie Aisch and mathematician Alfonso Rueda would have influenced him. He might have communicated with biologist Karl Pribam, Walter Schempp, Candace Pert, Stuart Hammeroff, Roger Penrose, David Peat, Fritz Albert Popp, or Rupert Sheldrake. The whole field of epigenetics would have amplified his theories. He might have had philosophical discussions with Merleau-Ponty.

"Jung in the 21st Century" focused first on the "mother science" of mathematics, which comes from the word "mater." Before the Great Plague and the splitting of matter and spirit in the West, number was understood to be an expression of Sophia, considered to be both the mathematical order of the universe (Wis. 11:12) and also its design, the *archetypus mundus.* In Her mathematical design of the universe and its manifestation Wisdom, Sophia, enacted Her role as both Logos and Eros. Later, medieval philosopher and theologian, Thomas Aquinas called these forms of knowing speculative knowledge and affective knowledge. Both types of knowledge are necessary for the formation of the universe and for synchronicity, "acts of creation in time," to occur. In the early 20th century the great Indian mathematician, Ramanujan, said that the mathematical foundations of the universe were revealed to him at night in dreams by the goddess Namakki. His work is only now being understood by mathematicians.

Dr. von Franz undertook a Herculean task in her book, *Number and Time*. She investigated number archetypes as the ordering factors active in both psyche and soma, finding that they have an inherent dynamical quality: *They represent abstract patterns of rhythmical behavior, or resonance.* Released from the merely quantitative role of scientific materialism, mathematics is now seen by many mathematicians as a symbolic language that is neither objective nor subjective but arises from the Imaginal realm.

Canada Post must have expedited my module on mathematics to Marion because the next afternoon she was on the phone, totally excited. "This is brilliant, you are brilliant, Elinor." She repeated this statement three times, as three, being the dynamic number, symbolizes bringing something new into consciousness. Since thinking is my inferior function, she was humorously trying to make sure I got it! We discussed mathematics not only as an abstract concept but as the ordering principle in chaos, the ongoing creativity of Sophia. That is, while Sophia, Wisdom, always plays in the Imaginal realm between the manifest and unmanifest worlds, the new mathematics, biology, and physics also arise from that same realm. The new science bears witness to the dynamic pulse of Sophia's creativity!

There is a dream image that analyst Edward Edinger presented both in his book *The Creation of Consciousness*, and in a lecture given in Toronto in the 1980's. In both dreams, although the context is slightly different, the central image is that of an enormous bird, the spirit, or breath, hovering over the waters. This is an image referencing the Old Testament book of Genesis. In the beginning we are told, "darkness covered the abyss, and the spirit of God was stirring above the waters." (Gen. I:2). What fascinated me was, that in each case, on the underside of the wings are numbers! The unconscious can express itself in dreams with such finesse.

Marion thought that New College might be a place where I could share some of these ideas. I did present two possibilities for courses that I thought might fit their program but there didn't seem to be any interest—and, of course, there was red tape. In retrospect, the first course "Jung in the 21st Century" with all its preparation was probably biting off more than I could chew. The second one, *Where Three*

Dreams Cross: Rising from the Ashes of Patriarchy is in the process of becoming a book. On the other hand, I was reminded again that Sophia has her own agenda and my efforts did not entirely go to waste. I unexpectedly received a phone call from my personal physician who teaches in the University of Toronto Medical School/Graduate and Fellowship Program. Would I lecture on Epigenetic Medicine? Some input from me close to the beginning of the course as to the psychological perspective could loosen up the boundaries. For five years this helped me maintain a focal point for thinking about the body that I did presented as: "Light Shining through Crystal." A mechanistic understanding of the body is long gone. Today, the body is seen more as a laser-like superconductor sending and receiving information at the speed of light. In fact, we are Light and Sound moving in and out of every cell. Researchers are beginning to discover the major function of our DNA has more to do with bioacoustic and bioelectric signaling rather than just protein synthesis. Similarly, our genetic makeup can no longer be considered deterministic; many things, such as exercise, nutrition, and feelings, can alter its expression. I brought in experiments showing how negative and positive feelings can alter our DNA, with perhaps Love being the most important element in any cure. As in earlier days, Marion wanted to come to Toronto to listen in on one of my lectures, but this was not possible given her current health restrictions.

Foremost, Marion considered herself a teacher, and so she was very interested in my reflections on a section I entitled "Healing the University." My starting point was the dreams of Nobel Prize–winning physicist, Wolfgang Pauli, in which he was invited to chair a new university, one that would combine both the notes and the music. Besides physics, psychology, and a neutral language (number), he felt a fourth element was needed, which he called *Eros.* For Pauli, this Eros light, the *lumen naturae*, is the light hidden in nature and springs from strong emotions.

With its binding power of attraction, most scientists would dismiss bringing such a radical concept as Eros into the University. Indeed, Pauli, in the 1950s, seems to have hesitated, because he thought it was too early and would ruin his reputation. To bring Eros into the university would throw the reductionist hold of reality into a tailspin. On arriving at this place, I found myself heaving a sigh, but then I began to think of the journey to retrieve the exiled soul that is happening on so many fronts and started to smile. Even Darwin recognized that emotion is the fundamental principle of evolution. In epigenetic medicine the feelings of the mother during pregnancy can change DNA expression, and experiments at Heart Math show that the feelings of the researcher can change the DNA they are dealing with. The connection between observer and observed generates effects well beyond physics experiments. Albert Fritz Popp demonstrated that the most essential stores of light, or biophoton emissions, are stored in the DNA. The work of Candace Pert shows how the molecules of emotion define the inforealm that constantly moves between psyche and soma, changing one into the other. Eros, the *lumen naturae*, has already slipped through the door of the "new university."

It seems to me that the ability of the University in preparing people for the 21st century and beyond requires an underlying reorientation based on Wisdom: Logos and Eros, Reason and Feeling, Intelligence and Beauty, understood both within and without. Influenced by the work of physicist Charles Card and analyst Anthony Stevens, I am convinced that universities need to be guided by a new Philosophy of Nature; an *Archetypal* Philosophy of Nature.

One of those who laid the groundwork for a philosophy of nature was the pre-Socratic scholar and scientist, Anaximander of Miletus (612-545 BCE). His book, *On Nature,* makes the first comprehensive attempt to bring together theories from cosmology to biology. While he is credited with the first theory of evolution, his most compelling insight established the *tension of opposites* necessary for creation to manifest. Through reflecting on the opposites, he came to the *Apeiron,* the unbounded and undetermined infinite that was transcendent but also contained the law of the world. That is, while containing the hidden laws of the universe, the *Apeiron* is both the source, out of which everything manifests, but also the unifier. This early formulation of the Self/Sophia from a philosophical, scientific point of view is the *arche*-type of everything existent within the unlimited, invisible *Aperion.*

From Anaximander to Descartes, the Philosophy of Nature was the heartbeat of most universities or schools of learning. Up to the 18th century, the Philosophy of Nature was based mainly on Aristotle's four different causes, or principles: material and efficient causality and formal and final causality. He argued that all four causes had to be present when attempting to explain any given thing. It was not until Francis Bacon that philosophy became split. Bacon did not reject Aristotle, but he argued that natural philosophy should be divided. Physics should deal with material and efficient causality, and meta-physics with formal and final causality. By the end of the 19th century, natural philosophy became a philosophy of science, based on Newtonian physics. The separation of mind and matter was complete. The scientific method of measurement and statistical analysis predominated. The notion of causality was reduced to its common usage as efficient causality, the analysis of things within the world of time and space. The problem is, when you separate psyche from soma, or matter from spirit, you may have what is deemed progress, but transformation is no longer possible.

When we morphed from a Philosophy of Nature to a Philosophy of Science, not only were the social sciences set aside but biology and chemistry were also set aside in favor of the principle of physics. Today all these sciences are becoming interwoven in ways that compel us into a new understanding of nature. More importantly, all these sciences are becoming recognized as a reflection of the archetypal depths of our psyche. Not only are biology and chemistry restoring an archetypal basis, but I was surprised to learn how many inroads into the sciences are taking place, including those dependent on the nonlinear behavior captured by powerful computers. For example, Dr. K. Mani Chandy, head of the Archetype Working Group at the California Institute of Technology, is developing an archetypal format to computer programming in an attempt to unify sequential, parallel, and distributed approaches. Many other studies, ranging from the development of language to prenatal development now recognize the underlying archetypal pattern.

Once we recognize the psyche and its dynamic interplay between conscious and unconscious, ego and Self, or between spirit and matter, we can begin to entertain a new vision. The unconscious, undifferentiated unity from which we emerged wants to become a more conscious, differentiated unity through us. Physics, chemistry, biology, linear complex dynamics, art, literature, music, theatre are all rooted in the archetypal dynamics of the psyche. In other words, *the psyche is the world manifesting through the sensual body.* To engage our world constructively in the 21st century we must bring to bear the hidden potential within ourselves in order to consciously shape a future capable of playing on the side of life.

Given the tension of opposites, several new schools and movements have been established, trying to address this imbalance between matter and spirit, psyche and soma, particularly as we realize a deeper understanding of what a participatory universe means. At New College, Marion inaugurated the daylong Speaker's Series that drew large crowds. The first speaker was Anthony Stevens, a psychiatrist and Jungian analyst, is well-known for exploring the connections between Jung's archetypes and evolutionary disciplines, such as ethology and sociobiology. The morning consisted of input from Stevens and in the afternoon he and Marion explored the biological aspect of the archetype together. Following the same format, other series included physicist Victor Mansfield and biologist Rupert Sheldrake, who explored the extended mind, the consciousness to be found in all of creation. Other speakers included a neurobiologist and a deeper explanation of what was happening at the cellular level.

Likewise, the Jungian Studies program that Marion was instrumental in founding at New College has blossomed. According to their website, the students took the initiative and founded a University of Toronto student-run Jung Society which is still going strong. They run events, discussion groups, film nights, and for the last four years have resumed the daylong conference.

Marion's pioneering work at Pacifica Graduate Institute laid the foundation for bringing in both a mature Eros and a mature Logos as a foundation stone for their programs. The founding president of Pacifica, Dr. Stephen Aizenstat, comments on her role: "Marion's keen interest in the conversations between mind and body, between spirit and matter, and most importantly between the authentic masculine and the authentic feminine gives value to Pacifica, and in turn, asks that Pacifica value not only the many demands of institutional and corporate life, but the stirrings of the deep psyche as well. Her call for knowing the inner reaches of a deeper Logos (masculine principle) and the expansive breath of a full-bodied Eros (feminine principle) offers guidance to an institution that is dedicated to sustaining itself as soul-centered in a culture dominated by corporate values."[28]

Education must go beyond the accumulation and manipulation of facts when we remember that archetypal patterns arise from the implicate order, the unbroken wholeness behind all reality giving rise to the fundamental dynamical patterns of Eros and Logos, chaos and order, representing both mental and physical processes. Education must include all the senses, particularly authentic feeling, necessary to play any meaningful role in our further evolution, both individually and collectively.

Marion was involved in education at many levels, including the Ontario Institute of Education at the University of Toronto. On June 4th and 5th 2007, the University of Toronto Centre for Diversity in Counselling & Psychotherapy sponsored a two-day seminar entitled "Dialogue with the Body." Workshops were presented in areas of traditional, alternative, and Indigenous healing practices including energy healing and working with images and symbols. The final evening of this event was the occasion to honor Marion with a Life Achievement Award from the University of Toronto. Amidst a beautiful setting of flowers and a live string quartet, Ross and I watched while Marion accepted her award. For me, it seemed particularly appropriate as 20-plus years earlier, this same large auditorium was packed, waiting for this new Jungian analyst in Toronto to speak.

I always feel a sense of joy at the recognition of Marion's work and, it seemed, as of late, many awards were bestowed upon her. I was particularly grateful that such recognition came at a time when Marion could receive it. She always accepted these awards with gratitude and grace, seeing them as affirmation of the task she was given to do in this life.

During this time, Marion also became acquainted with Professors Ed O'Sullivan and Eimear O'Neill, both of whom I call friends. On our

---

[28] Aizenstat, Stephen. (2005). In Appreciation of Marion. *Body & Soul: Honoring Marion Woodman, Spring Journal*, 87.

first meeting, Ed and I discovered that we were "disciples" of Thomas Berry. As Thomas had encouraged me to do in psychology what he was doing in theology, he had encouraged Ed to do the same things in education. Ed founded the Transformative Learning Centre at O.I.S.E., University of Toronto, and his book, published in 1999, *Transformative Learning: Educational Vision for the 21st Century,* was enthusiastically embraced around the world from Europe to China.

In 2006, Marion took part in the yearly gathering Ed and Eimear had at the University's Transformative Learning Center called Spirit Matters. Rooted in the vision of Thomas Berry, these four-day events were designed to further "The Great Work" of our time. In 2013, at the 20th Anniversary of the Transformative Learning Centre, I was invited to attend and be part of the weekend of celebration and emerging themes for the future. Former doctoral students and leaders in education from all over the world were there. Friday evening, in a large auditorium, we celebrated both past and future directions for the Centre through Emergent Theatre performances that included the audience. I remember riding home on the subway attired with streamers and a garland of flowers on my head. It happened to be Halloween, so I just blended in with the other revelers.

As we attempt to bring all aspects of ourselves into community with others and the planet, I remember a conversation Marion, Ross, and I had over tea in the garden at Sydenham. We were talking about all the ways that feminine energy was finding its way into the world, in science, in theology, in leadership, and in forms of capitalism beyond our patriarchal concept. As Ross pointed out, this energy is present but, for the most part, we haven't recognized it yet. Women are leading the way in embodying this new consciousness, and as they do, a new masculine energy is being born. The work that needs to continue is the work of Sophia in bringing a new heart-centered masculine Logos capable of holding the big picture, the larger meaning of the dance. A new vision is aching to be born. Sophia, as both Logos and Eros, is bringing together a new expression of Reality, but until we break through to the Wisdom and Love at the core of our own being we cannot fully act from that place.

Pictures of Marion and Elinor
at the post-investiture
gathering at Sydenham.

FOURTEEN

I would describe Sophia as an emerging archetypal pattern, not yet fully in consciousness that is bringing to our Western culture a new understanding of the relationship between spirit and matter.

Marion

In 1959, one of my three wise men, Thomas Merton, wrote about Sophia as "the Tao, the nameless pivot of all being and nature."[29] That is, as the eternal principle underlying the universe, the Tao is the source of being, non-being, and all transformation. In my early 20s, this introduction to Sophia did not really make inroads into my conscious understanding. Twenty-five years later, She would invade my consciousness in a much deeper way.

During my analysis in 1985, an enormous energy erupted from within me, and for one whole day I sat at my computer and typed out an eight-page monologue I called "The Song of Sophia." Up to this time, Sophia had not played a prominent role in my psyche, so I was quite startled by this sudden, all-consuming invasion of energy. I showed it to Marion who smiled but didn't say anything. Then I put it

---

[29] Pramuk, Christopher. (2009) *Sophia: The Hidden Christ of Thomas Merton,* (p. 194). Minnesota: Liturgical Press.

aside because I knew it was something I would have to grow into. It begins:

I am the Name of the Unnamable; the manifestation of Our glory. The name I speak is Wisdom; the Spirit of Truth spoken in love.

From the mouth of the Most High I came forth, and mist-like covered the earth. In the highest heavens did I dwell, my throne on a pillar of cloud. The vault of heaven I compassed alone, through the deep abyss I wandered. Over the waves of the sea, over all the land, over every people and nation I held sway. (Sirach 24: 1-6)

In my womb all things are created and by My breath they are sustained. Nothing has come into being except through Me, for Wisdom is Life. I sustain all worlds and direct their unfolding. I speak in the whirlwind, in the fecundating chaos, constantly yearning to give birth to the One. My house is in the depths of your being, and through you I invite all that exists to speak in the name of Wisdom. I am your life, your guide, and some day you will know me as you are known.

When I looked back to 1985 to what Marion had been working on during my analysis, I shouldn't have been surprised that this immense energy became galvanized in my unconscious. During my analysis we didn't have any discussions about Sophia, but I realize now that leading up to our encounter, Marion finally had the courage in 1982 to tell of the events surrounding her 40th birthday in India and her invitation to Krishna's birthday. She told about hailing a taxi and upon telling the driver she was invited to a celebration for Krishna's birthday he suddenly took off through the fields. When he stopped, the car was surrounded by men. Stepping out of the car, she was relieved of her camera, sandals, belt and purse. The men were looking intently at her and suddenly she was lifted above their heads chanting as they carried her to an altar. Since she had heard that human sacrifice still happened in India, Marion was sure this was to be her fate. She writes: "Convinced that I was about to be sacrificed, I was simultaneously dead and fiercely alive, quite beyond fear. I was receiving powerful energy from the men, a commingling of love and praise and awe. A man who seemed to be a priest put grass in my mouth, chanting with the others. He prayed over me. He took the grass and divided it among the men who ate it as if it were holy grass. They picked me up, put me on the altar and, again chanting performed a slow dance around me."[30]

Caught between fascination and fear, Marion reached a level of conscious surrender knowing that what was happening needed to happen. Through the chanting and ritual dance of those dark strangers Sophia reached out to her. "In that moment, that eternal moment, I heard her great I AM."[31] In celebrating Krishna's birthday, Marion had to confront her fear and her body image that were being burned away during the ritual. From some deep place, she knew this was an initiation into her destiny.

Although not named during my analysis, today I realize that the field between Marion and I had become sufficiently strong that her surrender and continuing initiation into Sophia's love had definitely played a part in opening my psyche. Writing about her experience allowed Sophia to burst forth in me, in both Her immanence and transcendence—and I suspect, many others. Now I understand Marion's smile. Even though nothing was said, I knew my life had just taken another turn on the spiral.

Marion's knowledge of Sophia grew as part of her own evolutionary journey, the expanded knowledge of which can be traced in her writings and talks. For Marion, "Sophia is the instantaneous illumination rising out of the icy water."[32] I remember that phrase "instantaneous illumination," as that is how I first *experienced* Sophia. What we both learned in our own way is that the more you surrender and allow the creative energy of Sophia to incarnate, the more you

---

[30] Woodman, Marion. (1985). *The Pregnant Virgin* (p. 180). Toronto: Inner City Books.

[31] Ibid., p. 181.

[32] Woodman, Marion, *Addiction*, op. cit., p. 75.

realize that your psyche encompasses the center that is everywhere and the circumference that is nowhere. To achieve a new standpoint in the world, one must surrender to that center, to stand at the still point and allow the creative energy to emerge. To be open to two worlds is not easy to achieve. Paradoxically, one needs a strong, flexible ego to be able to surrender, and not simply be overwhelmed and dissolve into undifferentiated chaos. In Marion's words, "the invisible center encountered in a creative process, at first not consciously recognized but gradually revealed as the process unfolds. That point, in other words *does not exist apart from the process; its being is always in the becoming, giving the process that assurance of its own reality...That continuous process within the eternal is what I think of as Sophia.*"[33] [Italics mine.] These are the words that reside indelibly in my mind. In surrendering to the process, we are becoming the incarnation of Sophia.

Through many guises, Goddess energy comes to us in our dreams and in our life. If She thinks you need to be chastised, She will do it; if you need a mother, She will hold you, but if She thinks you are ready to be a conscious instrument of creation, She will lead you into the depths of the underworld until you understand that the reality you think you know is really an illusion. If you follow Her to the depths, the ego's boundaries dissolve into the Void, or the Source, or, in my experience, the unbroken resonance of Love. Stripped from your habitual perception of the world, *what She is really teaching you is that Nature, including yourself, exists beyond time and space as energy, or patterns of probability that manifest in images and matter.* Once you surrender to the eternal moment, the world of time and space is given back to you, but you can never look at creation in the same way. You can no longer unconsciously live in the either/or world constructed by your ego, but you must hold the tension of a both/and world where everything is process. The repressed matter of your body must flow if you are to mirror the creativity of Nature rather than the concrete contours of materialism we so easily get caught in. In short,

---

[33] Ibid., p. 72-73.

you have been given inner vision or immortal eyes that penetrate to the essence of the One, spread across the universe, and know in that moment *you are that.*

Marion's understanding of our role in the creation of the universe is put so simply that I suspect many do not recognize its true import. She writes, "...in such moments, matter is seen not merely with our natural eyes, but is perceived with the inner eye. Perception requires imagination and creativity and reflection. When matter is *perceived*, the soul has created an image. The moment of perceiving concrete reality as an inner reality, as a soul-image, is a timeless moment, when the mundane meets the divine."[34] What we realize in those moments of seeing reality with our *inner eye* is that we are an instrument of creation. What dawns on us is how responsible we need to be for our images once we surrender to our role in creating the universe.

If we are to move beyond our stagnant, often destructive patterns, it is the mystic/shaman, surrendered to Wisdom's mantle of universal love, who can bridge the gap between matter and spirit; who can bring immanence and transcendence together as mirror reflections of one Reality. Seeing with the inner eye, the realization or incarnation of Reality is not a disembodied experience but requires the release and transformation of the patterns in the body/soul that the ego has reinforced in its need for control. In a world that has been reduced to its material components, the mystic breaks through to the numinous, transcendent background of reality, and in doing so, recovers the light in matter. She or he is then able to bring both the *Lumen Dei* and the *Lumen Naturae* together at the still point within the psyche. The numinous experience is like the parting of the veil, a glimpse into the world beyond our ordinary reality. As important as these experiences are, however, they are only a beginning, pointing

---

[34] Woodman & Dickson, *Dancing in the Flames*, op. cit., p.163.

to the necessary patterns within our body/soul that need to be made conscious and brought into balance. Working with the deep patterns of body and mind, releasing one into the other through the use of image and metaphor, is what Marion understood as the creation of the subtle body, or soul-breath; the non-material Life principle, animating both matter and spirit, raising not only the physical body to the Imaginal realm but all of creation. For the alchemists, this was the final *conjunctio* where body, soul, and spirit reunite with the world as a conscious reality; or in the words of the poet Rilke, "Earth, is not this what you want:/invisibly to rise within us?"[35] Today, hope lies in the fact that more and more people are piercing through to the experience of this state of Oneness, the metaphysical background beyond created reality that gives rise to both matter and spirit, making manifest the interconnectedness of all things.

As an archetypal pattern, Sophia has existed in many constellations of the goddess throughout humanity's short history. I think of the Book of Revelation 12:1. "And a great sign appeared in the heaven: a woman clothed with the sun, and the moon was under her feet and upon her head a crown of twelve stars." This points to an image of the cosmic Sophia, but we are told that, being with child She is driven out into the wilderness, which psychically is very true. Living at the margins of our consciousness, She gives birth to a Son whom the Beast comes to destroy. Two thousand years ago, the world was not ready for the new masculine, the Desirer-of-Life, to come into the world and so He is taken up into heaven, into the unconscious until the proper time. The question is, are we ready for him yet?

Following the Closing Ceremonies of the 2002 Olympic Games in Greece, Marion phoned. "Did you see that!" she exclaimed. Indeed, I had. In a huge stadium filled with futuristic innovations and

---

[35] Rilke, Ninth Diuno Elegy, op. cit.

technology twirling overhead, a young pregnant woman emerges as if from the underworld. Illumined by a single light, she wanders amidst all the activity going on around her. The commentators are at a loss of how to explain the significance of her appearance. The pregnant virgin was once more making her presence known. In our materialistic and technological modern world, do we really see her?

She is pouring out into the world through science whether we recognize her or not. She is an archetypal energy, a process that we can never fully know, invisible and always unfolding. However, as science penetrates the heart of matter the new images and metaphors that emerge help us to catch a glimpse of Her at work. For example, Medieval philosopher, John Scott Erigena (800-877) saw the *Sapienta Dei,* the Wisdom of God or Sophia as a "kind of primordial unity…that proliferates itself into numberless forms (archetypes), which at the same time nonetheless remain within the primordial unity."[36] Recently NASA's Chandra X-ray confirmed the findings of mathematical physicist Hartmut Mueller who, as Ervin Laszlo points out, found that the quantum vacuum, or zero-point field "is a cosmic ultra-weak background that acts as a morphogenetic field….Because the universe is finite, at the critical dimension points the waves [within the quantum] superpose and create enduring standing waves [that] by means of resonance… is responsible for the distribution of matter throughout the cosmos."[37] One day in the summer of 2015 I read that paragraph to Marion. She lit up, "I get that! Read more."

In the Old Testament we read, "Wisdom is mobile beyond all motion, and she penetrates and pervades all things by reason of her purity … the refulgence of eternal light … and she, who is one can do all things, and renews all things while herself perduring." (Wisdom 7:24-27) Similarly, 16th century philosopher Giordano Bruno saw the world soul as the love that runs through everything like a current or a light bringing everything into unity. With the advent of quantum

---

[36] von Franz, Marie Louise. (1992). *Psyche and Matter* (p. 914). Boston – London: Shambhala Publications.
[37] Laszlo, Ervin. (2004). *Science and the Akashic Field,* (p. 49-50). Rochester, Vermont: Inner Traditions.

theory, we have new metaphors for "the refulgence of eternal light." What science once discarded as a nuisance is now reclaimed as the cornerstone of a new understanding of the universe and our place in it. This "nuisance" we know as the zero-point-field, the lowest form of energy that is left after you subtract everything else. The quantum vacuum is really a quantum plenum, an underlying sea of electro-magnetic waves connecting everything in the universe, although as the lowest energy state it is unobservable. Astrophysicist Bernard Haisch explains, "We see things by way of contrast. The eye works by letting light fall on the otherwise dark retina. But if the eye was filled with light, there would be no darkness to afford a contrast. The zero-point field is such a blinding light. *Since it is everywhere, inside and outside of us, permeating every atom in our bodies, we are effectively blind to it*...it blinds us to its presence. The world of light that we do see is all the rest of the light that is over and above the zero-point field."[38] Since Fritz Albert Popp learned how to measure light in living tissue, we know that it resides in the core of our DNA; science has, essentially, brought back the *subtle body* or the *body of light*. The research of geneticist Mae Wan Ho found that the organism is coherent beyond our wildest dreams. Through her research she found that the liquid crystalline medium that pervades every part of the body, from organs to the interior of cells, allows for instant communication. Or, as stated above, Sophia, Wisdom penetrates and pervades all things by reason of her purity ... the refulgence of eternal light. While it would be a mistake to reduce Wisdom to the zero-point-field, we are now discovering new metaphors that bring the world within and the world without together, leading to a further trans-formation.

Medieval philosophers saw in the affective state of Eros the power of the soul to alter material things. Now, science has confirmed that emotions carry the information that acts simultaneously on psyche and soma changing one into the other and back again. This resonance captured Marion's attention many years before. The great

---

[38] Haisch, Bernard. (2006). *The God Theory* (p. 71). San Francisco, CA: Red Wheel/Weiser.

mystery is that consciousness, emerging through the archetypal patterns, reverberates in the cells of our body and in the vastness of space. We can study the development of self-organizing systems at every level of creation, and if we penetrate beyond the phenomenal world we recognize that the *self* in self-organizing is the evolutionary dynamic of Sophia in all her many manifestations.

What mystics know, have always known, is that the universe is within us. About 2,600 years ago, the Eastern world was shaped by a deep mystical tradition. In India, the Upanishads recognized the ground of all Being, Ultimate Reality, which they called Brahman, and the innermost essence of our own being which they called Atman. This transcendent reality, both cosmological and psychological, they would eventually refer to as the Self, perhaps best described in the Chandogya manuscript as "Thou are that." This truth has echoed across many centuries. In the 13th century, the Sufi mystic poet Rumi writes of "the entire universe inside you."

As the psyche is complementary in nature, it is not surprising that at the height of the Industrial Revolution and the reductionist thinking prevalent in the 19th century, Europe was introduced to the writings of the Upanishads. On the other hand, it seems we have largely forgotten our own roots. Going back 2,600 years, before Plato and Socrates, we find in the philosophical works of Empedocles, Parmenides, and Pythagoras the Western world was equally shaped, not only by a deep mystical tradition, but one rooted in the goddess. In his inspired epic poem, Parmenides not only articulates a mystical understanding of the world but, as philosopher/mystic Peter Kingsley points out: "Every single figure Parmenides encounters in his poem is a woman or a girl. Even the animals are female, and he's taught by a goddess. The universe he describes is a feminine one."[39] What the

---

[39] Kingsley, Peter. (1999). *In the Dark Places of Wisdom* (p. 49). Point Reyes, California: The Golden Sufi Center.

goddess teaches Parmenides is that his destiny is tied up with "the destiny of everything, the fate of reality ... Parmenides is being invited to participate actively and consciously in the origins of the universe."[40] Similarly, Kingsley tells us that the whole point of Empedocles' teaching is to learn to perceive consciously (with the inner eye). "And if you cooperate with this process you will soon make an extraordinary discovery—that the source not only of your own existence but of absolutely everything else's existence as well, now lies inside your-self."[41] Or, in our participatory world, Jung realized that "our psyche is set up in accord with the structure of the universe, and what happens in the macrocosm likewise happens in the infinitesimal and most subjective reaches of the psyche."[42]

If philosophers, poets and analysts can agree that the universe in inside us, a provocative question is, "has science advanced far enough to support their experience?" The physicist, John Wheeler, famously believed that there is no "out there" out there. That is, he rejected the notion of the universe as a machine, as something entirely separate from us and subject to fixed *a priori* laws. As he saw it, we live in a participatory universe; the universe explains observers, and observers explain the universe. In proposing a participatory universe, Wheeler concludes that, "any pre-life Earth would have existed in an indeterminate state, like Schrodinger's cat. Once an observer exists, the aspects of the universe under observation become forced to resolve into one state, a state that includes a seemingly pre-life Earth. This means that a pre-life universe can only exist *retroactively* after the fact of consciousness."[43] Wheeler was able to demonstrate this scientifically with a delayed-choice experiment. Carroll Alley and his colleagues would carry out this experiment, even further concluding that, indeed, Wheeler was right and what the experimenter chooses to observe today can shape the nature of reality (particle or wave) from a very long time ago.

[40] Kingsley, Peter. *Reality* (p. 169). Point Reyes, California: The Golden Sufi Center.
[41] Kingsley, Ibid., p. 554.
[42] Jung, Carl. (1965). *Memories, Dreams, Reflections* (p. 335). New York, New York: Vintage Books.
[43] Lanza, MD, Robert & Berman, Bob. (2009). *Biocentrism* (p. 80). Texas: BenBella Books.

Since there is no "objective" science, we cannot solve the ultimate mystery of the cosmos because we, the observer, are a necessary part of the equation. Having some experience as to what Reality looks like from the still point I remember one discussion Marion and I had around this subject. Marion had just returned from giving a keynote address at the Noetics Society. As I understand it, astronaut and scientist Edgar Mitchell had brought up remarks he made in *The Way of the Explorer,* namely that if we placed a sentient observer at the zero point, "looking at the macro world from beyond space-time, the observer should perceive the exchanges of energy in the underlying structure in electrodynamic balance, and in resonance with the Self, experience the connectedness of all things."[44] Jung equally struggled with the old question: does the world of ordinary reality exist if it is not observed? For Jung, the Self is an absolute, subjectless, supra-intelligence residing in the collective unconscious or we might say today, in the zero-point field of information. From this point of view, the Self/Sophia is the observer who collapses the wave function and gives birth to a universe.

When we spent time exploring such topics, it was not a dry, intellectual exercise. Looking back, such conversations were ultimately rooted in attempts to understand our own experiences, to bring together the world within and the world without. Perhaps the closest *experience* we can have as cosmic observer is that moment of Self-realization, or satori, when we stand in the timeless moment that intersects time; where the deepest point of interiority is also a cosmology; where the dancer is the dance.

Many leading scientists now seem to agree that time and space may be an illusion. It has become apparent that somewhere in the vicinity of the Planck scale, conventional notions of space and time do not really apply. That is, science is encountering the fact that space and time belong to the manifest world, a relative world defining ordinary reality. Sophia, residing in the *unus imaginalis,* the world

---

[44] Mitchell, Edgar. (2008). *The Way of the Explorer (Revised Edition)* (p. 208). New Jersey: Career Press.

situated between the subjective and objective worlds, has opened all science, including psychology, to the world of possibility, the world of images out of which all creativity comes. It is the world that comes into existence every time electromagnetic energy hits our senses.

Jung wrote: "The psyche is the world's pivot: not only is it the one great condition for the existence of a world at all, it is also intervention in the existing natural order, and no one can say with certainty where this intervention will end. ...We must emphasize that the smallest alteration in the psychic factor, if it be an alteration of principle, is of the utmost significance as regards our knowledge of the world and the picture we make of it. The integration of un-conscious contents into consciousness, which is the main endeavor of analytic psychology, is just such an alteration of principle, in that it does away with the sovereignty of the subjective ego-consciousness and confronts it with unconscious collective contents."[45] *That is, every time we bring the unknown contents of the unconscious, objective psyche into consciousness, the perception of the world is simultaneously altered.*

We are co-creators of the universe, but to be truly conscious of that reality we need to be able to open ourselves to the perspective of the Self. In a participatory universe, Jung has said that the world hangs on a string and that string is the psyche of man. More specifically at this moment, I think our future depends on the depth of our encounter with Sophia, the eternal process within creation. By penetrating the world beyond space and time, we can bring forth the self-organizing images capable of healing the many dualities that keep us estranged from ourselves and the world without. Science, in its essence, is a spiritual journey into the heart of matter and, like any spiritual discipline, science, with its new images and metaphors, is challenging the ego to go beyond itself. At this time specifically, we are challenged to go into the feminine way of presence and process, allowing new forms to appear.

---

[45] Jung, Carl. Collected Works, Vol. 8, par. 217

Sometimes people are surprised when they discover that most of the science in *Dancing in the Flames* was written by Marion, while the dreams, case studies, and historical context comprise most of my writing. For some reason, they assume it is the other way around. In alluding to *Dancing,* in 2005, Marion's husband Ross remarked that physics cast a powerful shadow on Marion's work without, as yet, being fully absorbed in it. As she often told Ross, physics absorption into her life and work is what she conceived as her final book. Von Franz felt that there would come a point when science becomes part of the individuation process and not a preoccupation of our conscious intelligence. That is, science would become embodied as an expression of one Reality. Given Marion's grasp of the metaphysical background beyond spirit/matter and the embodied depths which she plumbed, I felt this work would have brought us further into the reality of one world than we have so far ventured. Unfortunately, it was a work that did not happen and, in my opinion, is a great loss.

Deeply embedded in our commitment to Sophia, our friendship became a container in which many of the new patterns emerging in the world within and without could be held and shared. While we must live our own lives and be responsible for our own images and thoughts, there are moments when I miss playing in the land of three times ten with such an embodied, intuitive, and brilliant mind that instinctively goes to essence.

FIFTEEN

There was a tragic film made years ago which showed the devastation wreaked by the 1945 atomic bomb on the Pacific. Great sea turtles, instead of following their natural archetypal patterns to the sea, turned and went inland to find water. They died there in the sand. I just sat there in the theatre and cried.

Marion

Marion's tears were not sentimental. She understood the full import of what she was seeing. The inseparable link between the destruction of the planet and our own individual destruction increasingly played a huge part in her psyche. Coming from the viewpoint of addiction, it was an inevitable leap for Marion to see how our behaviors are throwing the patterns and rhythms laid down by Nature into disarray resulting in a dying into death. The earth isn't functioning the way it was meant to, and we have no guide, no compass to steer by. The full impact of the above image hits us when we realize that cut off from the psychoid archetype with its instinctual patterns at one end and spiritual patterns at the other end, we have severed ourselves from the evolutionary trajectory that has brought us this far.

Our relationship with nature often takes on a deeper meaning as we get older. Perhaps embarking on the final season of life brings that relationship into stark relief. No longer able to engage nature outwardly in ways we once did, I think both Marion and I instinctively entered into a deeper, inner ecology, moving toward that final *conjunctio* when body, soul, and spirit become one with the world. Everything in nature has an archetype within it that directs its growth and behavior, its material aspect and its spiritual aspect. Unfortunately, many of the images leading us to the numinous realm of the objective psyche have, in our culture, become increasingly disembodied and banal, reduced to advertising slogans. They no longer allow us to see the relationship, the interconnectedness of our lived experience. Likewise, cut off from our instinctual roots, like the great sea turtle, we can no longer find our way to the life-giving waters. While the spirit continues to create new forms and images, we remain possessed by matter in all its addictive forms: money, drugs, sex, war, greed, the suffering being born by nature itself. Living in a participatory world, Marion points out that if the body is "disassociated from the physical energetic field of the archetype; it has done so because the Earth is so full of unnatural pollutants that it no longer carries the pure archetypal energy for us to relate to."[46] In turn, the archetypal energies within our bodies are "misguided," resulting not only in the breakdown of our immune systems but a breakdown in the immune system of the earth.

Since the archetypes link us to our evolutionary history, to the beginnings of life in the universe, our DNA resonates with the original patterns of creation. Nature, uncontaminated by man, is capable of healing itself, and if we consciously embrace its self-organizing dynamic, it can heal us and our culture. For me, it is why the times spent in wilderness always feel like coming home. It's ironic that we evolved within an enriched, diverse planet suited to our needs, but through war, greed, and neglect we are turning it into a wasteland. Now many people see our salvation in going to a hostile wasteland such as Mars and trying to make it habitable. There is always the chance that we will learn humility relating to such a stark landscape,

---

[46] Ryley, Nancy. (1998). *The Forsaken Garden* (p. 109). Wheaton, IL: The Theosophical Publishing House.

but, at the moment, our ego, with its need to conquer, is still leading the way.

My former mentor, Thomas Berry, articulates the problem when he writes: "Having lost touch with the archetypal images means that we have lost touch with the genetically-coded source of our connectedness to the universe...It's the world of the archetypes which guides us in building a viable culture."[47] Our genetic and cultural coding when linked through the archetypal realm, shimmers with the numinous resonance of the sacred. Whether we stay on earth or dream of other planets to inhabit, the question remains: if we are going to build a viable culture, how do we get back to the guiding energy of the archetypal world?

Ecology was another passion Marion and I shared as integral to all that we were trying to embody. That is, any sustained effort to "fix things out there" must be rooted in the ecology of our own body/soul knowing that the universe exists within and is reflected through us. Ultimately, to talk about ecology is to resonate with the ongoing rhythm and revelation of Sophia, the creative matrix behind all manifestation.

In building a viable culture, an earth community, **one major path** well known to both Marion and me has been to work with the images generated by body/soul. We are nature and so we need to pay attention to the archetypal energy in the patterns presented in both our dreams and our body. This personal work is essential if we are to understand in what way we are being asked to become co-creators of the universe. The more we can open to the kairos moments in our life, the moments when the timeless intersects time, the more we are able to incarnate Wisdom as the Intelligence and Beauty informing a new story that wants to be told.

Having experienced Reality as a single vibration of Love, my passion has been to find ways to incarnate that vibration, the resonant source of creation on both a personal and transpersonal level. It will only be through the opening to feminine consciousness in women and

---

[47] Ibid., p. 248.

in men, that Love can enter the creative process. That experience was captured by Marion many years ago: "Once we're in connection with that Love coming through our own cells, then we can feel the suffering in the cells of the tree, in other people, in the planet. We recognize Oneness. Then we simply cannot violate the earth."[48] Through the integrated compassionate energies of masculine and feminine, Logos and Eros, we can begin to build a global earth community.

A **second** way to restore the reality of archetypal energy, which Marion and I both loved to explore, is through science. Although many scientists remain unconscious of their role, they are the instruments of a new shamanism and a new alchemy. In fact, in dreams they often show up as shamans in white coats. Having broken its reductionist shackles, science is able to probe the heart of matter and the heart of the universe into infinity, affirming Jung's understanding of the dynamics of the psyche and the dynamics of nature as one reality.

The great patterns in the natural world are the patterns revealed in the archetypes. We never see the archetypes, we can only experience them through images processed in and through the body. The ultraviolet (spirit) and infrared (matter) of electromagnetic energy defining the available spectrum of archetypal energy has, at the cultural level, become split, particularly in the last 500 years. The immense chasm we experience between matter and spirit has become so great that a reversal or upheaval is now taking place. The binding force of the *lumen naturae* has been rediscovered. Light, stored in our DNA resonates with the original patterns of creations, while its coherence throughout the body informs every molecule, directing and guiding it. If toxicity breaks down that coherence, disease can occur. The more we weave the images, old and new, from the past and the evolving future, a new story is emerging. Incarnation continues. At a personal level, we are aware of energy so immense we can barely comprehend it. It can snuff us out in a heartbeat, and yet, for Incarnation to reach its full potential, it needs our co-

---

[48] Ibid., p. 105.

operation, or more importantly, our conscious surrender to a greater Wholeness.

A **third** way capable of piercing through to the sacred container of creation is in our growing awareness of the wisdom of Indigenous cultures. Working with my Indigenous Anglo-Saxon/ Celtic roots [see pp. 111-114] deepened my own awareness. A few years ago, I was asked to give an opening address at a gathering in Toronto as a way of introducing Diane Longboat, a Mohawk ceremonial and spiritual leader, to support her upcoming journey. Diane had been invited by the Jung Institute in Zurich to speak and conduct ceremonies as part of their program. The obvious connection I made was between Jung's trip from Zurich in 1925, to Taos, New Mexico, and the Pueblo Indians, where his discussions with Mountain Lake had a profound effect on him. Right up to the time of his death 35 years later, Jung spoke of needing a self-understanding similar to that of the Pueblo people. Now, more than 87 years later, the sacred ceremony was going from North America to Zurich. Not only Diane's teachings, but also the ceremony of truth and reconciliation she brought to Jung's gravesite, had a numinous effect on all those present.

As Indigenous civilizations heal themselves from the soul wounds we Euro-Americans have inflicted upon them, they are rediscovering their spiritual roots, practices, and beliefs that embody the sacredness of the universe. If we are open, they can teach us how to listen to the universe, how to detect the patterns hidden in nature, how to bring our own lost past into the present. When asked to speak to an assembly of Canadian First Peoples gathered at Georgian Bay, Berry admits he didn't know what to say, so he went outside and sat by the water and asked the moon, the wind, and the earth. What he heard was: "Tell them the story, the story of the wind, and the river, and the bay. Tell them their story, the universe story."

The next morning Berry got up to speak: "What I say here is not important. What the stars say is important. What the wind says is important. What the river says, what the ocean says, all of this is important."[49] After his talk, the Mohawk chief said he had never before heard a white man speak in the voice of the grandfathers.

Along with physicist Brian Swimme, Berry did write a new creation story, *The Universe Story.* In it he describes the journey of the monarch butterfly. How the migration can be so long that the butterfly that returns is the grandchild of the butterfly that left two years before. "How does it know where to return to if it's never been there? How does it know to go to this specific grove, to this specific tree?" It knows because:

> The winds speak to the butterfly, the taste of the water speaks to the butterfly, the shape of the leaf speaks to the butterfly and offers a guidance that resonates with the wisdom [consciousness] coded into the butterfly's being.[50]

The reality embodied in this image takes me back to my time on Georgian Bay; the yearly canoe trips with Marcella and Eldon and Marion and Ross's Indigenous island of Sha Sha where I dreamt of the image of the butterfly tree. But archetypal images never exhaust what they can teach us. Released from the bonds of disembodied rationality, what I continue to learn is the butterfly, my body/soul, is guided by the landscape. Flowing out from the landscape of my body, through the landscape of my culture to the landscape of the world around me, the depths of that guidance is becoming clearer. From the beginning, our psyche, our emotions, and our thoughts, have been shaped by the landscape, the earth, the plants, the animals. The complementary consciousness in all of nature has informed our own, but we have become deaf to its voice. Thinking we are apart from the Earth's rhythm and patterns, we have lost our ability to live in a reciprocal relationship with it. It is only when our inner ecology becomes clearer that, like Marion's tears for the Great Turtle, we hear the cry of our soul weeping for the toxicity we have imposed upon it.

---

[49] Ryley, Nancy. *Forsaken Garden,* op. cit., p. 260.
[50] Ibid., p. 259.

If we return to the still point, to Sophia as the creative matrix in the depths of our psyche, we realize that everything in the universe can be our guide. One year, at the end of my course on Jung, the students at The Integral Healing Centre put up banners around the room containing sentences that I, apparently, am fond of repeating. The most prominent one stated, "The universe conspires to support the soul." That saying came years before, in Africa when those little parasites took it upon themselves to teach me how to surrender to a power greater than myself. Our birth, our life, everything that comes our way, is designed to support our destiny—if we do not get in the way. If we do not cling to our wounds but learn to walk through them, Wisdom will follow.

In 2015, I took part in a third conference with Diane and the Soul of the Mother people: *Returning to our Origins: Reconciling with our Indigenous Roots.* Certainly, reconciliation needs to take place between Indigenous Nations and the many immigrants who made their way to America. Five hundred years ago, and particularly in the last 200 years, the Indigenous Nations on this side of the Atlantic were cut off from their nature-based worldview through expansionism and Christian missionaries, particularly through the horror of Residential Schools that dragged children out of their homes and their culture, often desecrating their bodies and thereby scarring their souls.

Around the world, particularly in Europe and the Americas, we have forgotten our own Indigenous roots. In Europe, roughly 1,200 years ago, we were cut off from the nature-based worldview of our ancestors through the expansion of secular societies and Christian missionaries. Expansionism fueled by the exploitation and control of nature came with us to the New World. Psychologically, the rejection of the Indigenous Nations we discovered in this new place is rooted in the rejection of our own natural selves that was repressed many centuries before. We must support and celebrate the healing of Indigenous Nations today for their sake, for the sake of the earth, and for our own sake. That is, we all need to allow the forgotten roots of our connection to the earth to heal us.

One question that occurred to me was "what was lost in being cut off from a nature-based worldview?" What immediately came into my consciousness was the fact that *in casting off the nature-based wisdom of the past, we lost our ability to truly live in resonance with the emerging worldview of the 21st century, including the scientific worldview.* Since our ancestors were so deeply rooted in nature, they lived in a world of non-local causality, a synchronistic world rooted beyond time and space. They lived in harmony with nature recognizing its infinite source. This is the world that science is discovering but tends to think of only in abstract concepts. To embody this new worldview, we need to bring our experience of both the natural laws and the spiritual laws together into our lives—beyond personally embodying the revelation of our latest scientific discoveries that embodiment must extend to our way of life, to all our institutions, to our economic and cultural structures. For Marion and me, weaving these three major elements, bringing the inner and outer, past and future, together into an exploration of a new, emerging worldview became major threads in the tapestry of our friendship.

I am aware that Thomas Berry has slipped into the conversation and upon reflection I think it is because he meant a great deal to both of us, particularly me. The old saying, "when the student is ready, the teacher appears," could easily apply to my journey between 1979 and 1984. At that time, Thomas influenced many of the insights that would guide my future work, but it was also a period of preparation for the dreams that would lead me to my next important teacher, Marion.

Out of his ongoing development in bringing spirit and matter, masculine and feminine together, in 1997, Berry wrote *Dream of the Earth*. This was a book Marion couldn't put down. "Here, at last, is a man who understands process, paradox, receptivity, surrender, the glory of diversity in the unity of the Earth."[51] Marion worked with many insightful men as did I, but there was something in the life and work of Thomas, a mystic, a scholar, and man of nature, whose life's threads were in many ways resonant with our own. She was delighted when asked if she would step in for Berry at a large conference in

---

[51] Ibid., p. 75.

Toronto as he was not well. For me, it was equally delightful to have my two midlife gurus come together, as it were.

Given my experience in 1979, that the deepest point of interiority and cosmos are One, this quote of Thomas Berry served to affirm my experience over the years.

> We need a spirituality that emerges out of a reality deeper than ourselves, even deeper than life, a spirituality that is as deep as the earth process itself, a spirituality born out of the solar system and even out of the heavens beyond the solar system. There in the stars is where the primordial elements take shape in both their physical and psychic aspects. There is a certain triviality in any spiritual discipline that does not experience itself as supported by the spiritual as well as the physical dynamics of the entire cosmic-earth process. A spirituality is a mode of being in which not only the divine and the human commune with each other, but we discover ourselves in the universe and the universe discovers itself in us.[52]

If Berry's words opened me to embrace the immensity of love, Marion's words affirmed in me the intensity of love. Through Marion, I would learn how to commune within myself, with my own essence, while opening to the essence of the other. My moon-time dreams, so evident in my analysis, guided me in transforming the parts of myself that had lived in darkness. Through dreams and meditation, I recognized a more conscious need to let the energies of the body flow through the heart of Sophia.

In relating through the Self/Sophia, Jung recognized a form of love that "is not transference and not friendship in the usual sense... It is more primitive, more primordial, and more spiritual than anything

---

[52] Berry, Thomas. (1990). The Spirituality of the Earth. In Charles Birch, et al. (Eds.), *Liberating Life: Contemporary Approaches in Ecological Theology*, Marynoll, New York, Orbis Books, (pp. 151-158).

we are capable of describing."[53] Rooted in the timeless connection beyond ego desire, such love is able to embrace the unique Wholeness of the other: the light and the dark, the gift and the wound, the creative tension arising from all of Nature. On my 60th birthday card, Marion wrote this truth, so simple and profound: "I value your Being in my life. I value our dancing together. I love you, dear friend." Now, many years later, I see in these words the whole ecology of deep friendship, the rootedness in Source/Sophia, the dancing and spiraling outward, and the flow of love that goes far beyond itself.

In *The Pregnant Virgin,* Marion writes:

Surrender to the Spirit opens the virgin soul to the full range of Beingness, the carnal and spiritual passion that burns at one's center but is not personal. Recognition of the fire as nonpersonal allows personal ego desires to be burned clean. No longer identified with instincts or spirit, one is human, open to the love of Sophia and the fertility that comes through that love.[54]

While such love is not rooted in the personal, to be realized it must be experienced in the personal. The true measure of embodiment is the ability to recognize the essence of the other and of all creation in the flesh of the world. In the many ways, we mirrored each other; being challenged to grow into the experience of this love was the defining gift of our friendship. It was this love, coming through the cells of our body, that supported us in the everyday joys and challenges of life while supporting our individual destinies.

---

[53] Jung, C. G. (1973). *Letters, Volume I* (p. 373). Olten, Switzerland: Walter Verlag.
[54] Woodman, Marion. *Pregnant Virgin,* op. cit., p. 168.

PART IV

DESTINY AND
THE FINAL DANCE

SIXTEEN

**What I learned is the difference between destiny and fate.
We are all fated to die. Destiny is recognizing the radiance
of the soul that even when faced with human impossibility
loves all of life. Fate is the death we owe to Nature. Destiny
is the life we owe to soul.**

Marion

**Only in deep surrender to Sophia's choreography does our
destiny take shape.**

Elinor

Some people are aware of their calling early in life, while for many
others it comes in the middle years. In either case, it seems to me that
our destiny, while supported and carried forth by our gifts, more often
comes through our wounds. This was the case for Marion and me.

At age 50, Marion struggled with health problems and edema
that would lead her to Zurich. When we are open to the archetypal
depths, the soul can speak to us in very clear ways, often illuminating
where we are and where we are meant to go. The next stage of her
journey was made apparent in two very distinct dreams that Marion
often spoke about as shaping her journey and her life's work. In the
first dream, she is a temple priestess arranging a bouquet of red and
white flowers in preparation for a ritual. Light piercing through a hole

in the shape of a cross shines directly on a spot where the flowers are meant to go, but she cannot fit them into a holder. The dream reveals Marion's yearning for the light, but a voice says her prayers cannot ascend until she attends to the mess in the basement. She finds her way down a dark staircase and there, in a stagnant pool of water, she sees a black snake trying to get its head onto a large wheel, so the water can flow freely throughout the temple. The body is always trying to heal itself, but her instincts are locked into a futile task, leaving her body, her unacknowledged temple, suffering from acute edema. The snake is angry and strikes out at her.

This deep call to heal the split between spirit and matter, to turn her attention to the instinctual life, eventually leads to a second snake dream. While she is wandering through a wasteland, the black snake has transformed into a green and brown snake, the colors of the earth. This snake comes toward her, not on its belly but propelling itself upright as it approaches. It has a golden eye crowning its head. This snake leads her to a niche in a cave where there are two enormous books. She reaches for one, *The Seven Chronicles of the Western World.* The snake strikes her hand; it is not for her. A second book has a golden eye on its cover, the same golden eye that crowns the snake. She opens it. Inside, the pages are blank. This book has yet to be written. The only clue she is given comes from the unrestricted love pouring into her from the golden eye on the cover of the book. "This is your task," says the snake.

The first dream is personal pointing to the work Marion must do to integrate body and soul. The second dream is transpersonal. She is wandering in a wasteland which many acknowledge is a place we have arrived at today on a collective level. I see in this dream the message that the patriarchal age has exhausted itself and a whole new vision must be undertaken in which everything flows from the self-organizing feminine principle that reveals the wholeness of creation.

After her analysis with Dr. Bennett in England and four years at the Jung Institute in Zurich, the connection with the serpent in the basement cesspool was not yet fully integrated. That is, Marion wrote her thesis on Emily Dickinson, who she realized was equally obsessed with the light. Upon finishing her beautifully written thesis, she had a dream telling her now she could start her real thesis! She took that dream seriously and after pondering it for a while, she knew deep inside the *real* thesis she had to write needed to embody her own shadow energy. The dream was pointing to the fact that her disembodied shadow energy was what she had come to Zurich to heal. She wrote another entirely different thesis on eating disorders that became *The Owl was a Baker's Daughter.* With the publishing of her thesis in 1980, Marion embarked on the task of writing "the new book," beyond our present understanding of consciousness. Coming out of her wound, Marion's book garnered a huge response. By delving deep into her own shadow and daring to speak from that place, she had caught the pulse of a widespread emotional and psychic wound in many women living in a patriarchal world. From her wound came the opening to her destiny and the cornerstone of her legacy rooted in conscious femininity.

In 1996, the night *Dancing in the Flames* was launched, I made the comment that Marion is a poet who writes in prose style. *Addiction to Perfection* (1982*)* and *The Pregnant Virgin* (1984), like all her writing, are truly poetic and have the same effect as poetry. They bring together emotion, imagination and intellect, leaving the reader with a sense of wholeness, whether he or she immediately under-stands it or not. Marlene Schiwy wonderfully describes the experience of those who have read Woodman's books:

> At first it seemed I had stumbled across a new language and syntax, one which my mind was not sure it understood. My body, on the other hand prickled with excitement. It reverberated to the tuning fork of her words and recognized them as shockingly true, even familiar.[55]

What her reader's minds could not quite comprehend, their souls resonated with. Marion's writing is a tuning fork, so much so that

---

[55] Schiwy, Marlene. (2000). Saturating Language with Love: Variations in a Dream. *Reflections of Teachers at Midlife* (p. 31). New York, NY: Routledge Press.

many people who had never remembered their dreams suddenly find themselves dreaming after they encounter her work. I have had many clients complain that they can't recall their dreams. Inevitably, if I give them a copy of one of Marion's books, particularly *Addiction to Perfection* or *The Pregnant Virgin* they start remembering them. The soul awakens and recognizes itself in her words. During summers spent in the wildness of Sha Sha, resting on the ancient granite of the pre-Cambrian shield, Marion learned to speak and to write in the creative resonance of Sophia, the World Soul.

Early on, Marion realized that her language, both oral and written, was to be an instrument of consciousness. To achieve this balance, she would have to free herself from the linear, conceptual world contained in the disembodied structure of words. For weeks she tried to find a syntax that could simultaneously contain the passion of her heart and the analytic detachment of her mind. The unconscious suggested the way forward in a dream in which she is sitting by the shore of Georgian Bay trying to roll a lily pad (the Canadian lotus) into the shape of a cylinder pipe. To her dismay it keeps falling apart. She is distracted in this task as right behind her is an old hotel and on its balcony two men are fighting. The hotel, the old collective structures, symbolizes the patriarchal world with all its division and conflicts. Finally, one man throws the other off, right over Marion's head. She feels she must do something, but a voice inside just keeps repeating, "fashion your pipe." It reminds me of the final task the goddess Aphrodite gives to Psyche, who is instructed to keep her focus and not get caught up in rescuing others or trying to fix the present situation when her destiny is at stake.

In the dream, Marion looks down and beside her is a huge smiling frog proudly sitting beside a pool of green eggs. I love the image of the huge frog, perhaps one of the most chthonic symbols of the goddess we have. Suddenly, Marion understands that she is waiting for her to finish her pipe so the green eggs, the fertile gift of the watery depths can be formed into different sounds. In the "new" book Marion is to write, it seems that she will need an instrument capable of turning frog eggs into meaningful words if her destiny is to be fulfilled. That is, she is faced with finding a new syntax; one that would allow her to write about a process in motion that was still psychologically and scientifically credible in today's world.

In his study of language, philosopher Merleau-Ponty sees the "sensuous, perceptual world as primary. This wild participatory world, relational and web-like in character, *affirms the organic, interconnected structure of language as an extension or echo of the deeply interconnected matrix of sensorial reality itself.*"56 [Italics mine] Language needed for a "new" book has to be connected to our deepest sensorial reality, and it must come through the body, not just the mind.

Journeying deep into her own matter to learn the hidden language of her body/soul, Marion was able to embody a new language which took her beyond the codified language of the patriarchal paradigm in which we live. Through her surrender to the process within, Marion has brought successive generations of women and men into the knowledge of a conscious femininity, the necessary container from which the next stage of our evolutionary transformation can take place. The journey that Sophia was leading her on would reveal itself again and again in ascending and descending spirals, delving deeper and deeper into the mystery of creation—the dance between body and soul, spirit and matter.

My own destiny crystallized at age 57, when Marion and I were working on the galleys for *Dancing in the Flames.* Along with case studies of my clients and their dreams, I had included part of my own process in the book, particularly the time I was in analysis. Marion questioned me as to whether my soul was comfortable with putting the material out there. "Elinor, perhaps if you asked for a dream, you would get some indication?" The following morning, I awoke with a dream that had nothing to do with what I had written. My soul had already moved on.

---

56 Abram, David. (1996). *The Spell of the Sensuous* (p. 84). New York, New York: Vintage Books.

Marion arrived early the next morning, fortified with two Tim Horton muffins. As we sat down at my dining room table to resume our work, I told her my dream:

> *I am in a rugged, deserted place like northern Scotland. There are people standing around at the periphery, concentrating on a very deep abyss that had opened up. In the depths lived a great monster/dragon/beast that, even in the dark shadows I could see. Very slowly and carefully I was to bring the beast into the light of day so the water could flow again.*

Having no concerns about what I was to publish, my soul presented me with a dream that in many ways has consumed my life to this day. Marion commented that it was not a personal dream. She also smiled and said she was glad it was my dream and not hers!

It took a while before I could even approach that dream. The first thing I thought of was William Butler Yeats' poem, the "Second Coming," which ends with "and what rough beast/ its hour come round at last/ slouches toward Bethlehem to be born."[57] I understood intellectually that for a new dispensation to come into being, the transformation of human consciousness that so many are calling for, the Beast, the "weight of human history," must be brought into the light of day. I amplified the dream as much as possible: the mighty Leviathan shown to Job, the beast of Revelations who pursues the woman into the desert seeking to devour the new masculine consciousness, a medieval wood carving showing Christ as the bait to bring the Beast into consciousness. This latter image spoke to me because Christ is not the solar hero whose task it is to slay the dragon. Marion would remind me of Jung's understanding of the dragon as the god hidden in matter who must not be slain. In fact, Jung's *Answer to Job*, echoes Yeats' poem. The dragon/beast must find its way to Bethlehem; or in Jung's words, it must become the living redeemer. But what do you DO with that? Nothing, I decided, except meditate, be attentive, and above all, surrender to whatever process wants to flow through me.

---

[57] Yeats, William Butler. (1961). The Second Coming. In M. Mack et al. (Ed.) *Modern Poetry* (p. 75). Englewood Cliffs, New Jersey: Prentice Hall, Inc.

And what does it mean, "So the water can flow again?" To transform the wasteland, the damned-up potential for life in the collective unconscious needs to be released. Psychically, this is very frightening. With the ego in control, chaos is the enemy. But a new creation, a new transformation of consciousness requires the destruction of old structures. It is only out of chaos that new structures can come. We can try to slowly assimilate the beast, recognizing this energy in us, or it will get acted out in the world: in the exploding of hydrogen and smart bombs; in the vicious spectacle of terrorism. The chaos will come, consciously or unconsciously.

Gustave Dore's Painting of Leviathan. Gustave Doré, Public Domain.

All summer, I kept returning to this dream, but I was dealing with concepts. I didn't know what else I could do, but by October my dreams took an ominous turn. That is, on consecutive nights I began to dream of death—my death.

> *#1 A richly colored autumn leaf has fallen to the ground. In the dream I show it to Marion. She takes it and says we need to interpret this like a dream. It shows that my death is coming soon. (If the dream points to the death of the ego it is probably about transformation. If a plant or tree dies it might indicate actual death.)*

> *#2 My mother appears to me in a dream. (She'd died the month before.) She tells me I will die when I am 62. (I was 57 at the time.)*

For two years I lived wondering what would happen, but when I turned 59, the following dream image came to consciousness:

> *I am drowning in the ocean, but I manage to surface. There is no one around. I go down to the bottom a second time but then come up again. For a third time I go down but again I manage to surface. I know that if I go down a fourth time I will not come up. I manage to get to shore and pull myself onto a deserted, stony beach. I can only lie there exhausted.*

In this dream, the watery depths that the great beast was holding back became the churning ocean in which I had to struggle. The need to engage the overwhelming descent into chaos necessary to create a cosmos was becoming a lived reality. While being immersed in such chaotic forces three times suggests a baptism, there is a fine edge between new life and being pulled into a watery death. Death, psychic or actual, was very real. Given the archetypal symbol of the ocean, I intuitively knew this dream was a preparation for the task of bringing the great beast into the light. Again, I could only wait, resonating with the image of lying on a rocky beach totally exhausted.

Wedged between this dream and the foretold year of my death at 62, I celebrated my 60th birthday. At times it seemed almost surreal. I celebrated with my friends, Joan and Ron by sailing in the turbulent Strait of Hecate and exploring the mystic islands of Haida Gwaii. After a 24-hour turnaround I spent four days canoeing on Georgian Bay with Marcella and Eldon. It had been a while since I spent two weeks in the wilderness, but it seemed appropriate; a reengagement of my youthful Artemis self. In a less rugged tone, my family had a pool party with a wonderful cake prepared by my two young grand-nieces and nephew who made sure that it had lots of icing with gummie bears and sprinkles.

Then there was the surprise party and ritual that Sheila McCarry and Marion had prepared for me. Marion had to inform me the day before as I was to plan the ritual. I had no idea what to do but the night before I had a dream—or, at least, an image of the many-breasted Artemis, not as the goddess of wild places but as the mother of souls. I knew what to do, and like magic, the room prepared for the ritual perfectly fit the theme. There was an altar glowing with candles, and in front of it a large, red, birthing rug from Iran. Chairs were arranged along either side and forming an outer circle were enlarged images of the Mysteries at Pompeii that Marion loved so well. She led me in and I had a large open basket with long stem white roses in it. I arranged pictures of my mother and my grandmothers on the altar. It was a time to honor all the mothers in my life, those women, living and dead, who over the last 60 years had supported me, opened doors for me, and loved me into life. For each person, I put a white rose in the vase on the altar. I then gave roses to those around the circle and I talked of their role in my life finishing with Marion. I acknowledged that besides giving me the courage to be and accept myself, I learned early on that to be in relationship with Marion I had to come from a soul place. I was aware of the little smile on her face. Then it was time to break bread.

Birthday Celebration 1999.

Outwardly everything seemed fine. Inwardly, my 60th year was like a plateau. I felt that I had come to a place of balance, but the future seemed like a dense fog. This fallow place weighed on me. I remember discussing with Marion that perhaps I had gone as far as I could go in this lifetime. My 62nd year was approaching, and I wondered what would happen.

Psychically lying on that rocky beach, I could only surrender. From this place, I received a message from the deep unconscious telling me that there were four great spiritual cycles, and that I had lived through three of them and was being prepared for the fourth. While I had the same inner guide for many years, I had been given a new guide to see me through the fourth cycle. (It appeared as a Merlin-like figure.) I never know what to do with information like this and after six or seven months I thought, "Well, it is your life, so you should be able to figure out the first three cycles!!" Once I asked the question, what surfaced from my unconscious pointed first to the *knowledge* of Self. Next came the *experience* of Self and thirdly the *realization* of Self. In 1979, having glimpsed my own true essence where subject and object are completely absorbed into each other so that any sense of one's individual self disappears, I had experienced, in some measure, the *goal* of individuation. But, arriving at that goal, I understood that the real work had just begun. I realized the process from here on was about the conscious *incarnation* of Self. When I met Marion, I was given a friend who could both understand and support that process. Now, I began to realize that the death I was about to undergo entailed an even deeper surrender to the transpersonal energies that want to emerge.

I had another dream that I knew belonged directly to the underlying process of transformation my soul was engaged in.

I am looking out a large picture window at the back of my grandparents' house. In the yard outside, a lion and a tiger are whirling around in a circle slightly above the ground. They seem to be devouring each other. I watch in fascination, and then they disappear. Inside the house a young woman appears. She is reluctant to go out the front door as there are threatening figures outside.

179

On a personal level, I associate my English grandparents with the Victorian, patriarchal head-of-the-family scenario. During my childhood, my grandfather was loving but taciturn and stern. Now, in the dream, there is a large picture window in the back of their house exposing primitive energy undoubtedly repressed in the proper English household.

For the most part, I understand Jung most clearly when my experience takes me there, and the breakthrough to this dream came while reading *Mysterium Coniunctionis*. At a transpersonal level, the lion and the tiger represent the masculine and feminine principles, depicted as the thermiomorphic pair, structures of the old king and queen—the former paradigms that, in turn, determined our world-view. For a totally new worldview to emerge they need to return to their instinctual animal nature to be renewed. In Eastern symbolism, the lion or masculine yang principle, and the tiger or feminine yin principle are said to "drink and devour one another...Yang donates, and Yin receives. ...They mutually inspire and benefit."[58]

Returning to the instinctual life force is not a regression but rather a return to the energy necessary for a further transformation. When we are ruled within and without by a cultural script for a long time, that pattern becomes so familiar that we cannot envision anything else. Both at a personal and cultural level, great energy is necessary in order to break out and go beyond our familiar grasp of reality.

Sometime later, a second dream brought the opposites—matter and spirit—into play in a manner I could not totally take in.

I am in a large, open courtyard that seems to be in front of a church or cathedral. Two large adjoining banquet tables have been set up and there are people milling around. I look up and see high windows, like those in a gymnasium. Behind one window, the lion and the tiger lie together peacefully. A second window is slightly open, and an enormous five-foot

---

[58] Jung, Carl. (1974). *Mysterium Coniunctionis* (par. 404). Princeton, N.J.: Princeton University Press.

white bird appears attempting to come in. I am panic struck, and yell out, "Close the window!" even though the bird is so huge it could not have flown through it. Again, the scene shifts, and a body of water appears where the banquet tables used to be. A woman appears, a poet whom I knew some time ago; she suffers from a bipolar disorder. She says, "They want me to be a mystic" and then walks into the water until it rises over her head. Then she appears beside me and tells me she just wants to listen to country and western music.

The messianic banquet table is outside of any traditional, organized religious setting. The lion and the tiger, the instinctual energy of king and queen from my earlier dream have been reconciled. The Great Beast, the chthonic energy that I was to bring up from the center of the earth, constellated its polar opposite, the Great White Bird. Confronted with such energy I went back to Jung's *Mysterium Coniunctionis*. Sure enough, there he writes of the royal beasts, the lion and tiger, the yin and yang aspect as "a synonym for Mercurius (Hermes), or to be more accurate, for a stage in his transformation. He is the warm-blooded form of the devouring, predatory monster that first appears as the dragon. Usually the lion-form succeeds the dragon's death and eventual dismemberment [integration]. This is in turn followed by the eagle."[59]

Suddenly, I realized that the images in my dreams had begun to overlap. In my journey toward the incarnation of the Self/Sophia, I had encountered the heights and depths, matter and spirit, symbolized by the crocodile and the bird depicted in the judgment of Maat. The spiraling up and the spiraling down between the beast and the great white bird is now taken up at a greater transpersonal level of incarnation. As an alchemical symbol of the soul, it was Mercurius who constantly transforms matter into spirit and spirit into matter. He is also the *aqua permanens*, the eternal waters in which transformation

---

[59] Ibid., par. 404.

takes place. This was why I was instructed to bring the Great Beast into consciousness; so the waters of transformation could flow again. Being in the realm of the transpersonal I developed a deep awareness, not only for what Jung was trying to express, but also the difficulty it entailed for me and the reluctance on my part.

While both dreams seemed to speak to an alchemical trans-formation, I was aware that another, more personal, message was being conveyed. In the first dream, the young woman in her grand-parents' home was afraid to go out into the world. In real life, I did go out into the world and was on my own by the time I was seventeen. Desire for something, I knew not what, and sheer determination overcame my fear. Marion would remind me I was a survivor. Now, the primitive instincts are reconciled and peaceful in the second dream, but the reluctance is still there. It is the same reluctance I always had about going out into the world, but now the spiral has moved to the transpersonal realm. In the second dream, I would rather go unconscious (drown) than entertain the title of mystic. My friend, analyst Wendy Willmot confronted me with this tendency as a negative inflation. Rather than risk identifying with what was happening to me, a part of me would go in the opposite direction, blocking what needed to take place. What finally helped me understand and accept the message trying to come through was reading a passage in von Franz's book, *Archetypal Dimensions of the Psyche.* She writes:

> ...in other words, we can only integrate our personal shadow, not the collective shadow of the Self, the dark side of the Godhead. Yet if we suffer the problem of opposites to the utmost and accept it into ourselves we can some-times become a place in which the divine opposites can spontaneously come together.[60]

---

[60] von Franz, Marie Louise. (1999). *Archetypal Dimensions of the Psyche* (p.48). Boston – London: Shambhala Publications.

I found affirmation in that passage, a kind of "yes" moment not unlike my "yes" to the divine marriage over 35 years earlier. In its deepest polarity, the Self was trying to unite within me. While such power can never be identified with or even understood, I know I must be present to it, open myself to its possibilities, particularly at this time in history when we stand at the abyss between a dying world and one waiting to be born. Through all this, the weight of my shadow fell heavily on me, as it often does. Marion would just say, "We can only bow deeper and deeper to the ground." It is a burden we can sustain, once we realize that our life does not really belong to us. We can only *surrender* to the Life that wants to flow through us.

I often recognize the synchronicities manifested by this LIfe flowing through me. A few years ago, I attended an event at the University of Toronto where Cindy White, a Mohawk healer, was opening the session through drumming and singing. I sat there, and suddenly tears, copious tears, were streaming down my cheeks. This is not any normal response I would have. Later that evening, I mentioned this occurrence to Diane Longboat who spontaneously replied, "You have been visited by the ancestors. They have come to bless you." I sensed the deep truth of that statement, but it was something I had to ponder. Later, I was reading the newly published *Lament of the Dead: Psychology after Jung's Red Book,* a dialogue between James Hillman and Sonu Shamdasani. Hillman writes: "...this book is so crucial because it opens the door or the mouths of the dead. Jung calls attention to the one deep, missing part of our culture, which is the realm of the dead. The realm not just of your personal ancestors but the realm of the dead, the weight of human history, and what is the *real* repressed, and that is like a great monster, eating us from within and from below, and sapping our strength as a culture."[61] It was one of those moments when everything comes together: my "destiny" dream instructing me to bring the great monster/beast, "the weight of human history" up from the depths; the book I was working

---

[61] Hillman, James & Shamdansani, Sonu. (2013). *Lament of the Dead: Psychology after Jung's Red Book* (p.83). New York and London: W. W. Norton & Company.

on, *Where Three Dreams Cross,* an analysis of humanity and the need to bring forth the attributes of the soul, long buried in our history. Without this freeing of the light in such dense matter we cannot consciously embrace a new worldview rising out of the intersection of time with the timeless. Only then can we move forward into the future. For me personally, this was an affirmation about the way forward.

When I go on archeological digs in my filing cabinets, unexpected things always fall out. Perhaps I should not have been surprised that a note written by Marion in 2005 presented itself. In responding to my first attempt at an outline and themes for *Where Three Dreams Cross,* she was very enthusiastic about the work, and my ability to carry it off. Today, I can just laugh and say, "thank you, Marion."

Marion's life and work gives testimony to the old saying that the wound is where the light flows in. She was instructed to write a "new" book beyond the knowledge of our patriarchal history, and her struggle with the body uniquely allowed her to explore the untapped riches of the soma that Thomas Hanna called the great task of the 21st century. I can't think of Marion's work without thinking of Tor Norretrander's words: "Inside us, in the person who carries consciousness around, cognitive and mental processes take place that are far richer than consciousness can know or describe. Our bodies contain a fellowship with the surrounding world that passes right through us but is hidden from our consciousness. The body is part of a mighty living system, which totally forms and manages a planet that has caught fire."[62] By exploring the living bodily experience of women and men in today's world, she came to the creative core of feminine consciousness. The clarity she brought to articulating the emergence of this energy in women and in men was her great contribution to a world desperately cut off from Nature, a future where "progress" is so much more than the mere accumulation of matter.

My destiny was to bring the great beast, the "weight of human history," into consciousness. It seems to me now that our tasks are two aspects of the new story that allow the past and the future to

---

[62] Norretranders, Tor, (1999) *The User Illusion (410-411)* New York, N. Y., Penguin Books

converge at the still point; or, as philosopher Jean Gebser would say, the ever-present origin. The only thing that makes me a little sad is not being able to dance with Marion as in days past; moments in my writing when I stop to reflect, "What would Marion say about this?"

My journey has been an ever-expanding circumambulation of my satori experience in 1979, revealing to me the ways in which our deepest point of interiority is also a cosmology. It has taken me through the archetypal images in my dreams, to mythology and to science, where the density of matter has been blown apart by the findings of quantum physics, revealing once more the numinous creative matrix of the World Soul. By going deeper and deeper into the body, Marion came to the same place.

Known or Unknown, from the beginning we are all destined to be participants in the ongoing revelation of Sophia, the Creative Matrix that brings together spirit and matter. It is, as Marion says, the life we owe to the soul. We do not choose our destiny; it chooses us. From the womb we are formed for it and at our death it only continues. Our life is not really ours but an expression of Reality, and so it is a process. There is no point at which we can truly say it is accomplished as it continues to send out ripples within the vast field of our existence. What we can do is embrace it or not. We can turn to it; open ourselves to it; and above all, surrender ourselves to it. Beyond the fear that such energy may initially bring forth in us, what we are ultimately surrendering ourselves to is Wisdom, the distillation of beauty, truth, and love. Physics has made it clear that the message cannot be separate from the messenger. Since it is Sophia who makes our individual life task apparent to us in dreams and transrational experiences, our destiny cannot be accomplished without moving more deeply into Her vibration of love. Through my growing conscious awareness of the tension of opposites within me and in the world without, I have always tried to keep centered in the heart. More than anyone I have known, Marion lived from that place.

SEVENTEEN

What we consider extraordinary is only the ordinary informed by love.

Elinor

While Marion and I each had our own destiny that often required going our separate ways, our relationship played out within a larger field where synchronicities were abundant. This was particularly true during the latter years when letters and phone calls became our meeting place. Of course, Marion painted on a large canvas and letters and phone calls were always a major part of her life.

At the beginning of our friendship, I was a little taken aback, realizing that every day her mail was delivered in a bag. She would answer every letter even when, over the years, Ross and I would beg her to find a way of handling at least some of her mail more efficiently. She would just reply that she wanted to respond to each soul in love and this meant a hand-written note. The same was true for the answering machine and later voice mail. It was always full. As with her mail, each person would feel like they were the only one, and, indeed, in that moment, they were. For Marion, it was not only a balance between body and soul, but a balance informed by love between her soul and each soul she met.

Having such great energy, she often pushed her body beyond its limits. One Sunday evening I was going out for dinner with my friend, Peter. Before he picked me up, Marion phoned to give me some information. Ross had been visiting that weekend and had just left, but her voice sounded like something was physically wrong. I phoned Peter, who was a physician and asked him to bring his black bag with him. I assured him I was fine but thought I should drop by a friend's place before we went to the restaurant. I arrived at Marion's door, doctor in tow. It turned out she had pneumonia and the first signs of an irregular heartbeat. It took some time to find a pharmacy open on a Sunday evening and get things settled, but Peter was very patient. He had never met Marion, but he is very perceptive, and I remember him saying, "that woman doesn't have a mean bone in her body." While I had never thought about it that way, I could agree that she was very open and transparent.

Of course, that sensitivity to body and soul worked the other way also. I was shocked when Marion showed up on my doorstep one morning after she'd just finished a workshop and taken the red-eye from California to Toronto. At the workshop, she met up with a mutual friend who had phoned me that morning and subsequently told her I was ill. Somehow, the field between us was always intensified by any kind of stress.

On at least two occasions, a dream would inform me of Marion's distress. She thought it would be great if I attended an Intensive in the Carolinas. Knowing how important this work was to her, I wanted to share the experience with her, but it turned out that I couldn't go. The first night of the Intensive, I had a dream where Marion's soul appeared in the form of a dragonfly, wings beating almost imperceptibility fast. I held out my arm that had a royal purple cloth draped over it. The dragonfly alighted, and slowly turned into a butterfly, drifting off as free as the breeze. I got up thinking, "Marion is sick," which was the case. In a similar dream she was doing an Intensive on the West Coast and getting up early and working late into the night preparing a book for publication. Her admirable discipline could overtake her, leaving her soul exhausted. Marion would often tell me that I was her rock, her anchor, and it seemed this role applied even if we were 3,000 miles apart!

Other times I was very grateful to Sophia. When Marion's brother died, she had tried for hours to contact me by phone. Later, I learned that my answering machine was not functioning. At that stage in my life, I never read the newspaper obituaries but that morning, for some reason, I did. I saw the announcement of her brother's death and the Toronto funeral home where he was laid out. Thanking Sophia all the way, I rushed up to the funeral home where Marion fell into my arms.

Like many people, I received wonderful letters from Marion. Thinking back, I can remember a few that made me smile. One letter began, "I know I will see you in a few weeks for Christmas, but I want to talk to you <u>now</u> so I am writing this letter." What followed was a five-page letter on legal-sized paper with "private information" written vertically in the margin. I smiled because there was the telephone, but for Marion, writing was a way of processing what was on her mind.

In 2008, Marion spent her last day at her Walmer Road apartment. The movers were coming at 10 that morning so, for our last meal, I brought breakfast with me, en route, from Tim Horton's. In a stream of consciousness format I had written down the time she had spent meeting people there, the writing that flowed from her pen into books, articles, talks, and letters. I wrote of the times we shared life there; meetings and rituals with others and the countless meals and discussions we shared over the years. Although we had not spent any prolonged time together in the last few years, we both acknowledged that, over the years, we thought of each other every day. Conversation flowed as easily as it always did.

Marion was finding it difficult to leave Toronto. She had wanted to live there, and in the early 1980s, was keen to buy a waterfront condo in the Terminal Building. Ten years later, she wanted to buy a condo on St. Clair, east of Yonge Street overlooking a ravine, but neither happened. To ease her angst of leaving Toronto today, I suggested she could rent a suite at the Hilton overlooking the lake if she wanted to come up for the weekend or even a week. I lived nearby. I knew this would probably not happen, but the prospect greatly eased the move from Walmer Road. Finally, we had our own ritual bidding farewell to this space that had meant so much to her and, in many ways, to me. As words are often too fragile to bear the weight of what wants to be said, we stood in the hall gently holding each other until the elevator made its way to the 17th floor.

One of the last letters Marion wrote to me was on the eve of major surgery. "This is a sad little missive, but I need to connect to you." She was afraid of what the anesthetic might do to her. For me, this letter left me feeling sad and, I must admit, brought back a trace of anger in that if the health care in London some years before had not been so incompetent this operation would not be necessary. While the letters became less frequent, the phone calls continued. We would go right into soul and talk happily for a good hour, sharing as we always shared. Only around the edges were there indications that something was amiss.

Often the old synchronicity would kick in. That is, I would be at a gathering and the discussion would turn to Marion, or a small group of us who were meeting would bring our intentions for Marion to prayer. Arriving home, Marion would call on the phone. Analyst, Murray Stein had generously offered to read a manuscript entitled *Encounters with My-Self.* He wrote an email largely positive of my writing as a storyteller and then added, "More clearly than ever I can see what a strong figure Marion has been for so many. And I can see, too, that you have carried her work some steps further into our time."[63] His comments both surprised and pleased me. While I had mentioned Marion, I did not have a *conscious* intention to bring her work forward. True to form, as soon as I received the email, Marion phoned. I read Murray's remarks and how pleased I was regarding his comments about bringing her work forward but that I never consciously set out to do that. "Of course," she said. "We are psychically so close, it can't be otherwise. We dance at the still point together."

Not being physically present for much of the last five years often left me with some unease. For some time, Marion had talked about moving on, letting go, spiraling into a more introspective time in her

---

[63] Stein, Murray. (2013). Personal email.

life. In phone calls or letters, she would say things like wanting to drop into her own matrix, refining her images and giving time to allow new creative energy to come in. Approaching 80, she would talk of not wanting to be pinned down two or three years in advance, of wanting to live each day as it comes. Increasingly, she began to speak of being so overwhelmed that she was "walking on hot air." She felt her demanding schedule was against the feminine. Our conversations centered around bringing her role in the Intensives to an end. Over the last 12 years, we circled around this topic on at least two different occasions. She felt it was time for people to move into their own orbit of work in bringing others to consciousness. While she still had the energy, she wanted to write or focus on the programs at Pacifica and New College.

During this period, I wondered what was going on with the Foundation. I trusted those closest to her would pull her back into the reality of her body, if need be. I first realized that something was amiss when I received a phone call from her. Without saying hello, or any usual greeting, she said in an anxious voice, "Elinor, I can't be present anymore!" That was her biggest concern. Living in the present moment and relating to the other in that moment had become a way of life. Then she told me her dreams which were also distressing. In old age, I realized that the Intensives had become a container for her. She was being held in the loving dynamics of the group, in the work she knew so well, but there would be no moving out, no more new books. While her soul process was still so evident, the aging process would lead her into a new and unfamiliar landscape where order and chaos would take on a whole new, unexpected dynamic. I believe we all reach that moment where resilience and vulnerability become a daily dance as the body surrenders to soul.

The night before Ross's funeral in March of 2014, Marion was, understandably, very upset. Ann, Wendy, and I went over to see if we could support her. While the doctor had her quite sedated by this time, she recognized Ann and Wendy. Since I had not been physically present for some time, it took her a while to recognize me. When she did, as Ann said, "her whole body filled with joy." Marion almost cut off the circulation in my hands, she held them so tight. Even through the haze of her medication, I can still see those incredible eyes staring at me with such love. Every few minutes she would repeat, "We have such a deep relationship." If I had not been physically present for the past few years, I knew I had to be present now. I could feel her soul reaching out to me. Back in my hotel room that night I recalled Marion talking about the chrysalis, a favorite metaphor for transformation. She felt that life itself is a chrysalis where the essential essence of our being is preparing itself for the world into which it will be born when the physical body dies. Whatever would unfold, I understood that somehow my being here now was a call to bear witness to this final chrysalis experience. From the beginning of our relationship Marion, with her fierce intensity, would talk of being stripped down to one's naked reality; T. S. Eliot's "condition of complete simplicity/ costing not less than everything." While not being sure what it would mean, I knew, as much as possible, I had to be present to her emerging essence and what it needed to express.

The next morning my body/soul had its own "chaotic" reaction. I am so grateful to Ann Skinner who helped me process the angst coming out of the cells of my body: feeling I had denied for the last eight years that needed to be released in tears.

EIGHTEEN

An aged man is but a paltry thing,
A tattered coat upon a stick, unless
Soul clap its hands and sing, and louder sing
For every tatter in its mortal dress.

W. B. Yeats

In 1998, when *Coming Home to Myself* was published, Marion gave me a copy in which she wrote, "Dear, dear, Elinor with whom I know coming home." She saw me as I saw her: one of those companions, who having lived the aloneness of her own unique being, are part of a larger field of relationship made simpler by time. Home is closer than it once was. Death is making its presence felt; the diminishment, the aches and pains, and all that goes with the body's release of soul. Yeats's poem, which Marion loved to quote, rings even truer now for both of us. I drive my 17-year-old Honda and my 78-year-old body down the highway between Toronto and London. Weaving in and out of the ever-present trucks, I sometimes wonder if I will be "home" before her. Yet, I know this is what I am (want) to do.

While the body does become that "paltry thing," if the soul has had its way with us, if we have surrendered to its impulse, what we are left with are moments of NOW. For Marion, they "are not moments bound to the past, moments in which we experience ourselves as passive victims of our own fate. Nor are they moments bound to a future that will never come. They are moments in which the soul is, present tense, NOW, dancing in the flames."[64]

We must not live in denial, but in old age it is of little use to *focus* on "the tatters" that proclaim the passing of time. Witnessing and mirroring these last years of our friendship have been for me a very conscious leaning into soul meeting soul. Writing about our friendship has been a distillation of essence up to the present moment. Within the tapestry of this text, these are moments of beauty, of insight, of humor, and, above all, a joyous noise as soul clapped its hands and sang.

In our meetings over the last few years, while I was conscious of engaging her soul through the metaphoric realm of subtle body, my soul was fed as well. Some days she would hand me her well-marked, small book of Emily Dickinson's poetry with the request, "read to me." As I read the first few sentences, she would join in or maybe continue by herself. Poetry was in her bones and was her soul's expression. One day, our friend Wendy, having generously gone to get tea for us, came and sat down while we were reading. Marion explained to her that poetry, to really live, needs to be between two. She can read the poems on her own but when Love dances in the space between, they come alive.

Nearly 20 years ago, Marion said: "Once you surrender to the Soul you are in a totally different territory because you allow the transcendent to manifest through your body instinct...You are an instrument that's being used to animate the love that's coming through... Even in moments of anguish or loss...there's a glory to be expressed...but the glory is not disembodied, it is not in the future. For me, that glory to be expressed is the glory of a violet with a raindrop on it, or the glory of the pink on that cloud out there, or the clouds of glory surrounding a newborn baby. Or the fact that I can move my finger and know what it takes to move that finger. All these are miracles. Matter is sacred; the human and the Divine inter-woven."[65]

---

[64] Woodman & Dickson. *Dancing in the Flames,* op. cit., p. 165.
[65] Ryley, Nancy. *Forsaken Garden,* op. cit., p. 119.

These are some of the moments I have described throughout this book. They are not only moments of 20 years ago but moments of today when the timeless enters time. There is the moment sitting by the river, when Marion is caught by the majesty of a swan gliding by; the moment in the park where the color of the trees against a cloudless blue sky transfixes her; or the moment in the garden when the bright, contrasting colors of flowers fill her with beauty. As we sit there in deep resonance with everything around us, these are the moments she mirrors. They are moments when soul claps its hands and sings; the uncensored moments that reveal the authenticity of her life.

One day as we took turns reading this manuscript out loud, Marion exclaimed, "Oh, Elinor, you have been on a golden journey." "We have been on a golden journey," I replied. She nodded and smiled. These are moments I treasure.

In traversing the perimeter of the Garden, we come home to where we started and know the place for the first time. In the beginning, we are one with nature. As there is no clear distinction between the world within and the world without, there is no sharp division between conscious and unconscious. As Jung said, our unconscious lived in the landscape. To return home is to have traversed our evolutionary consciousness from purely instinctual through imaginal and emotional, to symbolic, and finally, mental realms. For me, this is the great archetypal "arc of transformation," with its descending and ascending patterns that can be traced through every level of creation, from atoms to molecules to humans. Humans have reached the bottom of that arc where world – body – soul – spirit, are all separate. We have managed to sort the seeds of evolution, but our discerning ego has arrived, only to forget the fathomless ocean on which it floats. Our collective journey is only half over. The unconscious depths need to be re-engaged and brought into a place of conscious awareness if further evolution is to occur. We need to bring back the lost faculties of the soul. Instinctual energies need to be transformed from their addiction to death, freed once more to become a *life* force propelling us forward. The magical ability of our Paleolithic ancestors needs to be brought into a new conscious understanding of the synchronistic experience of reality across space and time as well as our telepathic connection to the consciousness in all creation. Having separated out from our unconscious immersion in nature, we need to bring back the symbolic world of our early Greek ancestors that allowed our conscious perceptions to stay connected to the unconscious depths. Symbol and metaphor are channels allowing the greater consciousness to emerge. While the mental ego is essential in bringing home the treasures of the past, today, it is severely limited in its worldview by rationalism. The next great leap in consciousness will necessitate learning to surrender to the still point, to the greater circumference of the psyche, allowing new patterns to emerge. Only then can we embrace both the past and the future and bring them into a meaningful whole.

When the spaceless, timeless, egoless world of our ancestors returns with its conscious symbolic language, soul and spirit emerge. Without a container, spirit falls on hard ground, it can bring progress but not transformation. Progress without presence and process is an illusion. The soul with all its facilities restored becomes the creative container, allowing spirit to penetrate. This *conjunctio* becomes a matrix for life, bringing with it the restoration of the masculine *nous* (higher/extended mind), allowing us to see the deep interconnected-ness of all creation with greater transparency. Through embodiment, our ability for abstraction and higher mental functioning becomes harnessed to the service of the emerging Self/Sophia. This, it seems to me, is something of the essence of our shared life and work.

Opening to the unconscious depths and letting new life flow out through us can be a long process necessitating the deep work we have to do to release the destructive patterns in the body from the complexes and traumas it has endured. This can feel like death, the dismemberment that all spiritual traditions refer to. Through this death into life, the body is being transformed into subtle body, metaphoric body, or the body we now see as "light shining through crystal." The quantum body, now purified, is reunited with soul and spirit in a new constellation open to the archetypal world we came from. Archaic humans, living in the unstructured freedom of zero dimensionality, were one with the world, but it was not comprehended as such. At the corresponding end of the arc there is also an at-oneness with the world, but now experienced as a conscious reality. The unconscious is spread across the landscape once more, this time flowing through the conscious container of the heart. For Marion, "...the whole world has become the sacredness of matter...the life force is in the willow, the daisy, the chickadee, in everything. And we are part of that totality, part of that love. That is the Garden we return to. I feel that I have done the full circle."[66]

Unconditional Love is the currency of the soul that brings all things into relationship. Marion's capacity for love never diminished. Stripped of many things, her essence never faltered. In 2014, Marion was to move from a hospital-like setting to a suite that could accommodate her familiar desk and chair, her treasured books and wing-backed chairs for her visitors. These items, it seemed to me, were all the important material things in Marion's life at this time. I arrived at 9:30 a.m. to take her for a drive while the move was taking place. As I walked toward her room, nurses, aides, and volunteers were milling in the hall. "Are you here to take Marion?" "Yes," I replied. Two were crying, while another told me of her time at a workshop with Marion and Robert Bly. Another said how, according to her schedule, she arranged to have lunch or dinner with Marion, as there were not many people that Marion could talk to. Making my way down the hall, I was not sure I would get Marion out before the moving began, but I was sure that her capacity for love and her ability

[66] Ryley, Nancy. *Forsaken Garden,* op. cit., p. 119.

to bring out that love in others remained the untarnished essence of her being.

Through the body and the instinctual realms, Marion made her way and opened others to the possibility of that final *conjunctio*; the moment when body/soul/spirit once more becomes one with the world. For me, this is the eternal moment where the dancer and the dance become one. It is also the moment in which Marion and I shared our lives.

With these few words I have tried to articulate the experience of our friendship over the last 30-plus years. We lived and bore witness to each other within a field thick with resonance, in which every emotion had its part. Friendship rooted in Self/Sophia is always part of a larger field, and I would remind Marion how many people were thinking of her and praying for her; how many people loved her. She would say, "I know; I feel it right here," pointing to her heart. What I experience now, whether we are sitting in her room reading poetry, or sitting on a park bench at one with nature is the resonance of our relationship reaching beyond time.

The words of the poet Rilke come to mind:

> The inner – what is it?
> if not the intensified sky.
>   hurled through with birds and deep
>   with the winds of coming home.[67]

Home is just a breath away.

---

[67] Rilke, Rainer Marie. (1995). *Ahead of All Parting: The Selected Poetry and Prose of Rainer Marie Rilke,* trans. by Stephen Mitchell. New York, New York: Modern Library.

AUTHOR'S NOTE

On July 9, 2018, Marion passed from this life. Sitting on my sofa near the phone, I received news about her death a little after 10:00 a.m. Leaning back, I let my body/soul take in the moment. As I sat there with my eyes closed, Marion appeared as in a waking dream looking 25 years younger. I had no expectations, but I was not surprised by her presence. It was not a numinous encounter, rather the feelings were very familiar. It was more like we took up where we left off. Typical Marion!

In the dream, there are four conference tables arranged in an open square and we sit down together at one of the tables. Being four-sided, the square is often associated with wholeness, but as an enclosure with an open center it suggests a garden or a courtyard, or some other configuration often seen as a symbol of permanence and stability. In the hermetic and some Eastern traditions, the square is seen as stability, but the open center leaves room for the *anima mundi*, the world soul, that speaks to the interpenetration of heaven and earth. I give this short interpretation because the other prominent image in the dream is a 10" x 12" folder with a beautiful blue cover. This folder contains a "prospectus," a guiding statement about the need for a conscious feminine, but it is hovering above the table rather than taking its place at the center. The embodiment of this potential is to be the agenda for our discussions.

In my associations, the blue book symbolizes the "new" book that Marion was destined to write [p. 170]. Over the years, this book, beyond the Seven Chronicles of the Western World, would reveal the meaning and importance of feminine consciousness, both personally and collectively. Outwardly, feminism speaks to equality and its continuing, often hard-fought emergence is one of the hopeful signs in our world. Inwardly, feminine consciousness speaks to sovereignty as the fundamental core creative matrix that both women and men must be open to if we are to continue to evolve as a species. For Marion, the search for an ever deeper understanding of the meaning and realization of embodied, feminine consciousness and its meaning for the world was the work of a lifetime.

For me, a second image comes to mind. In my "friendship" dream, mentioned at the beginning of this book, I am lifted by the spirit and arrive at Jung's doorway. I go through Jung's office and arrive at the inner courtyard, which is Marion's office, with a grass floor and open to the sky. I have always understood her work not to be outside of Jung but at the heart of Jung. For Marion, the conscious feminine is present "in allowing the eternal essence to enter and experience the outer world through all the orifices of the body—seeing, smelling, hearing, tasting, touching—so that the soul grows during its time on earth... Soul-making is constantly confronting the paradox that an eternal being is dwelling in a temporal body."[68] The sacredness of matter, the release of soul, and the embodiment of a creative spirit was her passion.

In this current dream, a woman and three men, or two women and two men (I am not sure) dressed in business attire, come up to say they are withdrawing from this project. Sitting there, I could feel in my body Marion's disappointment, even grief, at their withdrawal. She turned to me and talked of the urgency and need for this "prospectus" to be embodied. Then she left.

The feminine energy at the center of all manifestation is being rejected by the broader world. To step into the real world in 2019 can bring on despair as we are assaulted daily with toxic, ego-driven agendas. On another level, we need only read the tributes and outpouring of love from around the world celebrating Marion's presence among us, calling us to rejoice in the positive energies that

---

[68] Sharp, Daryl and Woodman, Marion (eds.) (1993). *Conscious Femininity: Interviews with Marion Woodman* (pp. 134-135). Toronto, Ontario: Inner City Books.

are also being released. Marion would humbly acknowledge that love in death as she would have in life, but her *concern*, it seems, in leaving this life was the state of the world and the divisive, negative forces trying to pull us apart. While in the dream she felt sorrow over the current dysfunction in the world, among those inspired by her, one of the repeated statements I heard over the weeks following her death was in the form of a rededication to the Great Work that must continue with even more clarity and commitment in those of us left behind. The need to bring feminine consciousness to bear, in order that the masculine spirit might have a creative container in which to plant new seeds, is the tension of opposites we must hold to in these times.

What has become clearer to me is that the new dispensation can only come from the timeless realm. We cannot simply conceptualize the future as some type of linear progression. Emerging out of the mist, we once lived in a timeless world where the unconscious, unknown mystery of life was, in Jung's words, spread across the landscape. The relatively short span we call patriarchy equals a time of ego development necessary to articulate consciousness, but that time is over. The bandwidth of our ego is too narrow. Operating within the acknowledged limits of time and space, for a further leap in consciousness to occur we must open ourselves once more to the infinite. If we, and the earth, are to survive these apocalyptic times, the ego must surrender to a greater Reality. We are called to live from the depth of our Beingness where soul and spirit, heaven and earth intersect. If we can live from that place of intersection, then out of the container of our body/soul will emerge new ways of being and thinking. I find hope in the fact that this new, expanded consciousness is already taking shape in so many ways.

Marion and I had a relationship characterized by joy and creativity, but reading this manuscript over one more time, I am even more deeply aware of its rootedness in that timeless place. Given the need for *all* relationship to be rooted in this wider and deeper reality is, perhaps, one of the main reasons why, over the past four years, Marion was so insistent that I write about our friendship.

CPSIA information can be obtained
at www.ICGtesting.com
Printed in the USA
BVHW071625210319
543324BV00002B/63/P